The Indie G   Vegan Cookbook

Easy Gluten Free Vegan Meals

120 Recipes

Clare Cogbill

Cover design by Connor McMorran.

DEDICATION

For Alun, Connor and AnaMaria

- thank you all for being such an integral part of the dream.

Love you guys!

CONTENTS

ACKNOWLEDGMENTS

Thank you to my family and friends for being there to taste the disasters and the triumphs.
Thank you (again) to Connor McMorran for a wonderful book cover.

WHY VEGAN AND GLUTEN FREE?

Shortly after completing my previous vegan cookbook, my husband was diagnosed with coeliac disease; hence many of the foods we had eaten until then were suddenly no longer suitable for him. We found ourselves in a situation whereby we not only had to veganise any new recipes we came across or created, but also de-gluten old ones.

Anyone who has ever been unlucky enough to be presented with a coeliac diagnosis will know how difficult it can be to have to exclude gluten from your diet. There was never any inclination on Alun's behalf to be anything but vegan, so, having already been vegan since 2002, in 2016 we embarked on changing our diet to being gluten free vegan. Medical forms Alun had to complete to assess the calcium level of his diet had a dairy bias, something we both found incredibly frustrating. With a lack of options of vegan calcium-rich foods on the list he was presented with, he proceeded to add to the bottom of it all the lovely foods we vegans eat which are high in calcium (nuts, beans, dark green vegetables, tofu, plant milk, vegan yogurt etc.). We found ourselves being cross about a form and a system that seemingly did not recognize those calcium-rich vegan foods.

Gluten is present in so many foods. By comparison, eating vegan is one of the easiest things in the world – for the many years we have been vegan, we really have found it to be so much easier than being on a gluten free diet.

The health benefits of a vegan diet and, more importantly, the fact that you can eat with a clear conscience, are obvious to all those who follow this path. The concept of being vegan is, to us, black and white, there are no grey areas – you're either vegan or you're not. And additionally, for Alun's health, there can be no compromise regarding gluten free eating and avoiding contamination of foods with gluten.

But why vegan, why not just be vegetarian?

I had already been vegan for about eight or nine years when I witnessed a newborn calf being taken from her mother so that people could consume her mother's milk. That sickening feeling that I had just observed something I had known about for so long, and which I steadfastly disagreed with – the main reason I initially became vegan, is one of the most memorable moments of my life. I felt helpless – sick to the pit of my stomach. What should I have done? Should I have rushed into the field and screamed at the farmer and told him to give the calf back to its mother? But what use would it have done? Except to have possibly got me arrested. Instead, I drove the car along the road, parked up, and sat and sobbed and sobbed for the cow and her calf and the human-induced, barbaric severance of the maternal bond. And yet, this scene is played out across the world millions of times per year.

Apart from those first few hours when she gave her calf colostrum from her breast, the cow would never again be able nurture her baby – the calf would be fed through an artificial teat so that humans could drink her mother's milk. If female, the calf would finish up in the same endless, torturous cycle of pregnancy and milking predicament as her mother. If male, he may be killed immediately as unwanted waste from the dairy industry or, more commonly, enter the meat market and become veal, dying before six months of age. He may end up with a slightly longer life, much of it enclosed in a barn, never seeing a blade of grass except on his way to the slaughterhouse at around a year and a half of age.

A dairy cow has to have a calf in order to produce milk, that is a fact. That milk is designed for *her* baby. Surely there is something fundamentally wrong with one species consuming the milk of other animals. It is not only incredibly cruel, but it's bad for the environment, unnecessary, and not good for our health. Humans are the only species that drink milk into adulthood. There is absolutely no dietary need for it. And then to drink the milk of other species; milk that is designed to nourish offspring that could grow to be 500-1000 kg or more, there must be something extremely wrong with that? If people like the taste of milk, there really is a delicious plant milk for everyone.

It is not only cows and calves that suffer. At Easter time we see scenes of fluffy yellow chicks paraded across the media. What the fairytale chicks don't demonstrate is what happens behind the scenes to the little boy chicks. Male chicks are industry waste that are usually killed after hatching (by a multitude of means). Some may say what about free range eggs? Unfortunately few people, including most free range producers, want a load of cockerels running around causing mayhem? Egg farming itself is no party for the hen, whether or not they're free range. In addition to the male chick 'problem', cage-reared hens have all the issues associated with confinement, and free range egg layers have the same male chick issues. There is little market need for male chicks because the egg-laying breeds are not designed for meat.

To us as ethical vegans, the facts about milk and eggs are black and white. To us, the dairy and egg-laying industries are the tips of the icebergs which represent a way of eating which has for so long treated animals as commodities; to use and abuse for the sake of taste and money.

Regarding meat or fish, most people can immediately see that what appears on the plate is a dead animal, and why some would not want to eat them. When you say to someone that you're vegan, however, and vegan for ethical reasons, many fail to understand why. The questions then abound, with usually the top of the list being why milk and eggs are not okay. After all, the animal doesn't die, does it? Well, hopefully I've already answered that here.

To an ethical vegan there is no compromise; nothing that is 'okay if the animal is treated well' – this is a fairytale drummed up by an industry that wants people to think that if we treat animals well, they won't mind us eating or using them. This is the pinnacle of the problem which begins with the happy farmyard lies we are told when growing up – when meat is called by a name other than what it really is; when pigs are known as pork, and cows as beef; when animals are seen in children's books living happily without any of the eventual death of those animals. Stories leading to the slaughterhouse naturally don't make good reading for little children. And the slaughterhouse? Before anyone tries to trick any of us into thinking there is a happy, 'humane' ending there, I'd argue there really is no such thing as humane slaughter.

There are no fluffy endings in animal agriculture. The only possible happy ending is if that animal is lucky enough to eventually find itself in a well-run sanctuary – rescued from the jaws of being reared for food and by-products, and ultimate slaughter.

And so, we many years ago found ourselves as steadfast vegans, but we were then suddenly presented with this thing, coeliac disease, which, when we investigated, we found had a genetic link in Alun's family. Luckily the doctor he saw was quick to act and offered a tentative diagnosis pretty well straight away. Then, of course, Alun's blood test and the subsequent endoscope examination came back positive. Basically, in his case, his body reacts badly to the presence of gluten in foods. Gluten is a part of cereal crops such as rye, wheat, barley and spelt. It can also accidentally be present in food by contaminating other cereals. Gluten consists of proteins that make dough sticky and stretchy. In coeliac disease, the immune system treats gluten as though it is a foreign substance and attacks it in the digestive tract – in Alun's case causing severe pain (although people will vary in their reaction to gluten).

As someone without coeliac disease I don't need to be on a gluten free diet, however I've found that by excluding gluten I feel better – a lot of digestive system symptoms I previously had are much easier now. I imagine that somewhere along the way I may have developed some level of insensitivity to gluten, and finding out in this way has been one of those chance things that sometimes happen in life.

The time of the diagnosis was such a difficult one, and as we ploughed our way through re-examining food packets, this time for gluten as well as animal products, we discovered so many foods that contain gluten. I think soy sauce was our greatest shock! Veganism really has always been so simple for us; the gluten thing, however, was so much more difficult and became a huge learning curve. But we knew we had to get it right, because if we got it wrong he could have become extremely ill. Alun's reaction to gluten is manifested in the most awful abdominal pain (as I've already said, symptoms seem to vary between individuals). Once diagnosed, he very quickly came to know from his pain reaction whenever he had accidentally eaten something that contained or was contaminated with gluten, and there really is no compromise with this – he has to have a gluten free diet.

I hope this book will suit those on a budget, both in the initial purchase of the book and in the ingredients we use. The ingredients are found in most supermarkets.

Some may be curious about why there are black and white

photographs in the book. As an independent author I've found it incredibly frustrating how difficult it can be to get my work into the public domain, and the inclusion of colour photographs affects the price that the reader has to pay. This makes it difficult for me to be able to compete, when my print runs are much smaller than they are for large publishing companies that can print thousands of copies and distribute them into multiple outlets. I hope that when people go on to make the food, the taste of the recipes will speak for themselves. I have, however, only been able to include ten images within the text, again, to make it affordable and within my publishing means.

As my previous vegan cookbook has pretty much been priced out of the market through publishing costs, I've adapted some of the recipes from that book to make them gluten free and included them here, along with many more new recipes. Cakes have been a challenge – and I thought I'd never master the gluten free vegan cake – but what you'll find here are a variety of great cakes (and biscuits and energy balls) that are tasty and which have been tried several times.

As mentioned, the ingredients are fairly cheap – the biggest outlay with most vegans is usually in purchasing nuts. As a family, nuts without a doubt are the most expensive foods we buy! They are, however, so important to a vegan diet, and therefore a cost worth making a priority.

I hope you will support me in this venture and that, ultimately, you will enjoy making these recipes for yourself and your loved ones, safe in the knowledge that no animal has suffered in their creation. And from a gluten free perspective, you can be confident they are suitable for those who require a gluten free diet. Do continue to packet-check in the supermarket, though! Ingredients can change, and we have been caught out a few times by 'new recipe' labels that we've missed at the point of purchase.

Thank you so much for purchasing this book and supporting me in my spreading the word about how easy (and cheap) vegan gluten free food can be.

Vegan . . . for the animals, the environment, and health!

Clare

When our cupboards went from being regular vegan to being gluten free vegan

One thing we've noticed about converting from ordinary vegan to gluten free vegan is that we're probably eating much more healthily than ever. I think there can sometimes be a tendency even when vegan to succumb to the dark side and rely too much on vegan junk food. Being gluten free vegan means that, for the most part, you just can't do that – not very often anyway!

What I've done in the following few pages is to have gone through our old vegan cupboard/fridge, and noted some of the changes we had to make to create a vegan gluten free (vgf) food store. What's surprising is that because it's so difficult now to depend on 'fake meat' products for back-up, much of what we eat now comes from what we make – which makes it much cheaper. Probably only about ten percent of our main meals now originate from the world of pre-packages. So, here we go then – some information and advice which I hope will help:

The Fridge and Freezer

Plant milks – (rice, coconut, soya, almond, hemp, cashew etc.) and **plant milk products** such as vegan cream cheeses, vegan yogurts, creams and vegan cheese. The only one we have eliminated from a gluten free perspective has been oat milk. Being creatures of habit, however, Alun has stuck to rice milk (the plant milk he's always chosen) and me to soya. Luckily most of the vegan yogurts and vegan cream cheeses we use are soya or coconut-based, and hence seem to be gluten free. We just check the packet if we're unsure, or if we see those awful dreaded words 'new recipe'!

Vegan margarine – all the ones we've come across seem to be okay for coeliacs.

Olives – plain black, green, sliced – all fine. Just check, as all we vegans do, for the dodgy ones with bits of meat in them!

Salad – The one bizarre thing we've found with pre-packed salad is that it sometimes comes with bread croutons. Why, oh why? They also seem to wilt as soon as you look at them. Much better to get a lettuce, cucumber, tomatoes, carrots etc. and make your own.

Vegan sandwich slices – We used to buy these for a quick lunch or as a roll-filler to take into work, but unfortunately all the ones we've found have contained gluten!

Roll-out pastry – you can get a vegan gluten free version for when you fancy a quick sweet or savoury pie.

Vegan sausages and vegan burgers – there are a few varieties available that are vegan and gluten free, and we do tend to have a few packets in stock just in case we're in a rush. They are sometimes a little more expensive than regular vegan sausages and vegan burgers, which can be a bit annoying.

Frozen fruit – all good! It's great to have ingredients you don't have to worry about regarding animal products or gluten.

Soya mince or soya chunks – while there are many now for vegans, finding a gluten free version can be a bit trickier. The basic soya mince is generally okay though.

Tofu – all the ones we use are fine for coeliacs, but do check the packet just in case there is some dodgy marinade coating on it.

The (Our) Vegan Gluten Free Cupboard

Vegan chocolate – Yes, yes, yes! All the vegan ones we use are also gluten free, but we always check, especially the flavored ones, just in case.

Popcorn – Seems to be fine, but check the packet in case any odd additives or contamination, or make your own.

Vegan oatcakes and crackers – Very difficult to find ones that are suitable for those who have to be gluten free. Check the special allergy section at the supermarket, but take care because a lot of them contain honey and are therefore not suitable for vegans.

Nuts and seeds – we use as many varieties as our cupboard will hold! Mostly unsalted varieties, as you can incorporate them into many recipes. Take care, however, with dry-roasted nuts as they often contain gluten.

Grains – we mainly use rice (brown, white, or wild), but also quinoa, corn couscous or polenta. We had to ditch our old wheat couscous, which we used to love.

Pastas and noodles – Many of these are not suitable for gluten free diets, so, while you're looking out for eggs and milk on the ingredients list, you also need to check for gluten-containing ingredients. There are many 'pastas' now that are based on a variety of ingredients such as rice, beans and chickpeas. Amazing! And some are extremely tasty.

Vegetable stock – some vegetable stock cubes contain gluten, so it is wise to check the ingredients. To help, it will often say in the allergy box whether or not it contains gluten, alongside where it tells you whether it contains milk. Also, as always, do check there are no meat or fish ingredients.

Cans of beans and pulses – we keep lots and lots of varieties of beans in stock including adzuki, black-eyed, haricot, green lentils, kidney, broad bean, butter beans, chickpeas, sweetcorn. We tend to buy them canned in water rather than salt water to avoid unnecessary added salt intake – this also means that as they contain only beans and water, they don't contain gluten. Again, it's probably worth checking the tins to make sure there are no 'nasties' lingering.

Vegan mayonnaise – we've found with this and many sauces that we've had to be careful about whether they contain any wheat or barley. We even found one apparently safe one that said it was gluten free but which contained barley.

Soy sauce – This was the big shock for us. Even before Alun was diagnosed, we had friends over for dinner, one of whom is also coeliac. Luckily, before I splashed soy sauce into my tofu stir-fry I checked the ingredients, and there was wheat hiding away in the ingredients list. Luckily there's a vegan gluten free version that is available in most big supermarkets.

Jams and marmalades – most are okay.

Pickles, chutneys and sauces – That barley thing from the vinegar content is troublesome, resulting in lots of close scrutinisation of the ingredients section on the label. When I make chutneys I use cider vinegar or balsamic, but this unfortunately makes them expensive to make – better to make jam!

Yeast extracts – Most of these seem to be okay – again, check the label. Also be sure to keep a constant supply of nutritional yeast flakes for sprinkling on pasta, rice, casseroles etc.

Sugar – the usual vegan unrefined sugars should be okay. Alternatively, agave nectar or maple syrup are usually fine.

Vegetable oils – these should all be fine!

Breads – very difficult, but you can find gluten free vegan breads. You just have to scrutinize the gluten free bread and wrap packets and look for all the usual problems like milk, eggs and honey.

Peanut butter – all good and there are lots of different nut and seed butters now – perfect yummy gluten free vegan food.

Tahini – a paste made out of sesame seeds which is useful in dips and spreads, so all good.

Flour(s) – ordinary flours are obviously a big negative here. We tend to keep in stock gluten free plain, gluten free self-raising, and gluten free bread flours. We also keep in stock gram flour, coconut flour and rice flour. Polenta can be a good alternative too.

Herbs, spices, seasonings, essences – we tend to use fresh herbs as often as possible, but if they're not available, dried ones will be fine. Being vegetables, they're all fine. Just watch out for mixed seasonings just in case there's any hidden flour.

This list is by no means exhaustive, but they're the main ones I use:

- Oregano, marjoram, parsley, basil, thyme, sage, coriander, rosemary, and mixed herbs, herbes de Provence, or bouquet garni for lazy casserole days.
- Paprika, turmeric, chilli flakes, ground cumin, cumin seeds, cayenne, mustard seeds, black pepper, cardamom pods, bay leaves, garam masala, curry powder.
- For garlic and ginger I use fresh as much as possible, but dried

of either works okay.

- Vanilla pods, vanilla essence, peppermint essence, almond essence.

Alcohol – Even for vegans this can be a bit of a minefield, although it has improved a little in recent years with clearer labeling by the manufacturers. For gluten free vegans, most vegan wine is okay and many ciders, but beer can be a huge problem. There are gluten free beers, but not all of them are vegan! Anyway, for us this resulted in lots of internet-checking and packet reading. Now we tend to keep in vegan gluten free cider, wines, a couple of beers, and the occasional spirit. I don't drink at all, but some of these are invaluable for cooking sauces and in some desserts.

Fresh from the garden?

We are lucky enough to have a month or two of the year when we don't need to buy so many tomatoes, onions, potatoes, herbs, lettuce, spinach, courgettes, garlic, and various fruits, as we've found them relatively easy to grow.

Our tree fruit has been quite successful lately, even though the trees are still quite young. Growing food takes a bit of effort and a bit of space, but it is worth it! We don't have a massive garden, just a town garden, but we created a rule, food (organic) to be grown in the back garden, and flowers in the front.

The rest of the year we have to depend for all our vegetables and fruit on the local stores. We choose organic whenever we can, but we're just like most other families, in that if the organic version really is grossly over-priced, we go for the cheaper non-organic option.

And so, to the recipes. The following recipes are mainly the meals we make from day to day – the cakes and puddings we only have for special occasions. I truly hope you enjoy making them for yourselves.

Please note:

The acronym vgf, i.e. vegan gluten free, is used throughout the recipes.

The recipes are designed for:

Main meals 2 large portions

Soups 4 portions

Desserts for 6-8

Some Soups

Spicy Orange Chickpea Soup

What you need

2 cans of chickpeas

2 large oranges,

2 medium onions, peeled and chopped

3 medium sweet potatoes, peeled and cut into 2cm cubes

4 crushed garlic cloves

250ml vegan yogurt

2 tbsp rapeseed oil

500ml vegan gluten free (vgf) stock

1 tsp chilli flakes

1 tsp cumin seeds

1 tsp mustard seeds

½ tsp ground turmeric

1 tsp paprika to decorate

What to do

Grate the zest from the two oranges and then peel and chop them, removing any seeds and pith. Put the zest and chopped oranges to one side.

Fry the onions in the rapeseed oil for 4-5 minutes until softened. Add the chilli flakes, mustard seeds, turmeric and garlic and fry for another 2 minutes. Add the sweet potatoes, vgf stock, orange zest and chopped oranges and simmer for 7-8 minutes.

Add the vegan yogurt and chickpeas and simmer for another 7-8 minutes.

Serving suggestions

Serve without liquidizing, or liquidize if preferred. Sprinkle with smoked paprika .

Beany Sweet Potato Soup

What you need

2 leeks, chopped into 1 cm pieces

2 medium sweet potatoes, peeled and cut into 1 cm cubes

2 onions, chopped

1 can of chopped tomatoes

1 can of borlotti beans, drained

1 can of green lentils, drained

Rapeseed oil for frying

500ml vgf stock

1 tbsp agave nectar (if required)

1 tbsp tomato puree

1 handful of chopped fresh basil

What to do

Fry the onions and leeks in a little rapeseed oil for about 5 minutes, stirring frequently.

Add all the other ingredients except the basil and bring to the boil. Simmer for 15 minutes, stirring frequently.

Add the chopped basil and simmer for another 5 minutes.

Serve with a swirl of vegan cream.

Serving suggestions

Nice and hearty and can be a soup served with vgf rolls, or a casserole with boiled brown rice or mashed potatoes. Add a teaspoonful of chilli powder when simmering if you prefer something a little spicier!

Roasted Vegetable Soup

What you need

1 red pepper, sliced

1 orange pepper, sliced

2 extra-large (giant) tomatoes, cut into 1cm pieces

2 medium courgettes, halved lengthways and then cut into 1 cm slices

1 medium aubergine, cut into 1.5cm cubes

2 red onions, sliced

6 garlic cloves, crushed

2-3 tbsp olive oil

600ml vgf stock

Handful of chopped fresh chives and/or parsley

Salt and ground black pepper

What to do

Roast all the vegetables until lightly-charred (except the chives/parsley) – usually for about 20 minutes, turning them half way through. Add the garlic when the vegetables are turned over.

Remove the roasted vegetables from the oven and blitz them in a food processor with the chives and/or parsley. Place the liquid in a large saucepan and mix in the vgf stock, along with salt and pepper to taste. Simmer for 5-10 minutes and then reheat when needed, adding salt and/or pepper to taste.

Serving suggestions

Vgf rolls sliced, topped with meltable vegan cheese, and baked for 5-10 minutes until the vegan cheese has melted.

Green Bean and Edaname Soup

What you need

2 onions, chopped

100g fresh or frozen green beans

100g fresh or frozen butter beans

100g fresh or frozen broad beans

100g frozen peas

100g fresh or frozen edaname (soya) beans

A handful of mixed fresh herbs (e.g. parsley, oregano, marjoram)

600ml vgf stock

250ml vegan cream

1 tbsp rapeseed oil

Salt and ground pepper to taste

What to do

Gently fry the chopped onions in the rapeseed oil for 4-5 minutes, frequently stirring.

Add all the beans, the peas, the herbs and the vgf stock. Bring to the boil and then keep the pan covered while the soups simmers for 18-20 minutes.

Remove the soup from the heat and carefully blitz the bean mixture with a hand-held blender. Add the cream and simmer the soup for another 3-4 minutes until heated through.

Serving suggestions

Serve with vgf bread or potato wedges.

Onion, Very Garlic and Tofu Soup

What you need

1 block of tofu , cut into 1cm cubes

6 onions, finely chopped

The cloves of 2 garlic bulbs, crushed

3cm fresh ginger, grated

A handful of parsley and the leaves of 2 sprigs of rosemary, all finely chopped

2 tbsp vgf soy sauce

750ml vgf stock

What to do

Marinate the tofu in the soy sauce and bake on a well-oiled baking sheet until lightly-browned (turning often to prevent them from sticking to the sheet). Put the tofu to one side.

Fry the onions with the garlic and ginger, stirring regularly and taking care not to burn them. Add the vgf stock and the chopped parsley and rosemary and bring to the boil. Simmer for about 30 minutes.

Add the cooked tofu and simmer for another 3-4 minutes before serving.

Serving suggestions

Sprinkle linseeds, sunflower seeds, and pumpkin seeds over the soup for a crunchy extra protein and omega boost!

Springtime Black-eyed Bean Soup

What you need

1 bunch of spring onions, finely chopped

4 sticks of celery sliced and chopped into small squares

6 small carrots, halved lengthways and finely chopped

¼ of a dark green cabbage or a handful of black kale, finely chopped

2 cans of black-eyed beans, drained

1 tbsp sunflower oil for frying

750ml vgf stock

Salt, pepper and dried mixed herbs to taste.

What to do

Gently fry the chopped spring onions in the sunflower oil for 3-4 minutes.

Add the vgf stock, carrots, celery, and cabbage and bring to the boil. Simmer for 15-20 minutes.

Add the black-eyed beans and salt/pepper/dried mixed herbs to taste and simmer for another 8-10 minutes. Serve with the beans still whole, or blend with a hand blender for a nice thick soup.

Serving suggestions

Serve with vgf crusty rolls or with croutons made out of vgf brown bread which has been coated in vegan margarine and then baked on a baking tray until crispy.

Creamy Cauliflower and Artichoke Soup

What you need

2 onions, finely chopped

2 cauliflower heads, cut into florets and chopped

1 small green cabbage, sliced and finely chopped

1 jar of preserved artichokes, finely chopped

I can of coconut cream

750ml vgf stock

1 tbsp rapeseed oil for frying

1 tsp ground cumin

1 tsp smoked paprika

What to do

Gently fry the chopped onions in the rapeseed oil for 4-5 minutes, frequently stirring.

Place all the other ingredients in the pot, bring to the boil. Cover the pot with the lid and then gently simmer for 20-25 minutes.

Remove from the heat and carefully blend with a hand-held mixer.

Serving suggestions

Once served, sprinkle sesame seeds on top of the soup. Serve with brown, crust vgf rolls or vgf bread.

Rice Noodle and Tofu Soup

What you need

1 block of tofu, cut into 1cm cubes and marinated in soy sauce

1 red pepper, finely chopped

1 yellow pepper, finely chopped

6 spring onions, chopped into 2cm slices and then cut lengthways into sticks

1 small bag of fresh bean sprouts

1 red chilli, finely chopped

3cm ginger, grated

6 garlic cloves, crushed

750ml vgf stock

Packet of rice noodles (2 portions)

What to do

Marinate the tofu in the soy sauce and bake on a well-oiled baking sheet until lightly-browned (turning often to prevent them from sticking to the sheet). Put the tofu to one side.

Lightly fry the chopped peppers and spring onions fir 5-6 minutes, stirring regularly.

Add the chilli, ginger and garlic and fry for another 3-4 minutes. Add the vgf stock, bean sprouts, tofu cubes and noodles and simmer for another 5 minutes.

Serving Suggestions

Sprinkle with sesame seeds and serve with some vegan sushi and a small bowl of soy sauce.

Mushroom and Parsley Soup

What you need

400g mushrooms finely chopped

2 large onions finely chopped

750ml vgf stock

A 250ml carton of vegan cream

I tbsp rapeseed oil

3 cloves of garlic, crushed

Handful of fresh parsley, finely chopped

Small amount of fresh parsley to garnish

What to do

Fry the onions in the rapeseed oil for 4-5 minutes until they are softened.

Add the chopped mushrooms and crushed garlic and fry for a further 4-5 minutes, stirring regularly.

Add the vgf stock and simmer for 25 minutes.

Add the cream and chopped parsley and simmer for a further 4-5 minutes.

Blend the soup with a hand blender to make it nice and smooth.

Serving suggestions

Warmed crusty vgf rolls or vgf pitta breads cut into triangles (with vegan cheese melted on top for a special treat) and baked at 200 degrees Centigrade until lightly browned.

Easy Vegan Red Wine Tomato Soup

What you need

2 cans of plum/chopped tomatoes

3 finely chopped onions

200ml vegan red wine

3 cloves crushed garlic

500ml vgf stock

1 tbsp vegan margarine or 2 tbsp light olive oil

2 dstsp agave nectar (if you like your tomato soup to be sweet)

One handful of fresh basil, chopped

What to do

Fry the onions in the margarine or oil for 4-5 minutes until they are softened.

Add the wine and crushed garlic and simmer for about 3-4 minutes.

Add the two cans of tomatoes, the vgf stock and agave nectar (if required) and simmer for 15 minutes.

Add the basil and simmer for a further 3 minutes.

Blend if preferred.

Serving suggestions

Warmed vgf bread rolls and a swirl of vegan cream.

Red Onion Soup

What you need

4 medium, finely chopped red onions

2 medium, finely chopped brown onions

1 tbsp rapeseed oil

1 litre vgf stock

250ml vegan red wine

Handful of chopped fresh parsley

Pinch of black pepper

What to do

Gently fry the onions in the rapeseed oil for about 5 minutes until they're softened.

Add the wine and simmer for 5 minutes.

Add the vgf stock, parsley and black pepper and simmer for a further 30-35 minutes. The onions can take a while to properly soften.

Blend and serve.

Serving suggestions

Warm, wholegrain vgf bread rolls sliced in half and baked, coated in vegan cheese.

For vgf 'croutons' – simply cut two slices of granary bread (on which you've spread vegan margarine or oil) into small squares and bake for 5 minutes at 200°C. Sprinkle the squares on the soup before serving.
If you want 'cheesy' croutons, just sprinkle grated vegan cheese (and dried oregano) on the pieces of oiled bread before cutting into squares.

Spicy Sweet Potato Soup

What you need

4 medium sweet potatoes, cut into 1.5cm cubes

2 finely chopped medium onions

1 litre vgf stock

1 tbsp rapeseed oil

1 tsp curry powder mixed in a bowl with 1 tsp garam masala, 1 tsp cumin seeds and 1 tsp mustard seeds

Handful of chopped fresh coriander

What to do

Gently fry the onions in the margarine for 4-5 minutes until soft.

Add the curry powder and other spices and keep on stirring for 1-2 minutes.

Add the vgf stock and sweet potatoes, bring to the boil, and then simmer for 20 minutes.

Add the fresh coriander and simmer for a further 5 minutes.

Blend until it is nice and smooth.

Serving suggestions

Warmed vgf pitta bread triangles or vgf pizza bases made into garlic bread.

Lentil and Potato Soup

What you need

2 medium potatoes, peeled and cut into small cubes

8 medium sized carrots, grated

1 mug of lentils, washed

3 medium onions, finely chopped

1 litre vgf stock

2 tbsp vegan margarine

One handful of parsley, chopped

What to do

Gently fry the onions in the vegan margarine for 4-5 minutes until they're softened.

Add the potatoes, carrots and vgf stock and bring to the boil.

Add the washed lentils and simmer for 15-20 minutes.

Add the chopped parsley and simmer for a further 5 minutes.

Blend if preferred.

Serving suggestions

With warmed vgf pitta bread triangles, or warmed wholegrain vgf rolls

Lentil, Leek and Tomato Soup

What you need

2 medium potatoes, peeled and cut into small cubes

8 medium sized carrots, grated

1 mug of lentils, washed

2 medium leeks, finely chopped

1 can of chopped tomatoes

1 tbsp tomato puree

One handful of fresh mixed parsley, basil and oregano, chopped

2 tbsp rapeseed oil

1 litre vgf stock

What to do

In a large saucepan, gently fry the leeks in the rapeseed oil for 4-5 minutes until they are softened.

Add the potatoes, carrots, washed lentils and vgf stock and bring to the boil, leaving to simmer for 20-25 minutes.

Add the chopped parsley, basil, oregano, tomatoes and tomato puree and simmer for a further 5 minutes. Blend before serving.

Serving suggestions

Warmed vgf pitta bread triangles or warm, crusty vgf bread rolls

Minty Broccoli and Pea Soup

What you need

1 broccoli head, chopped

2 large onions finely chopped

500g frozen peas

200ml of soya cream

1 litre of vgf stock

1 tbsp rapeseed oil

10 mint leaves, chopped

What to do

Gently fry the onions in the rapeseed oil for about 5 minutes until they are softened.

Add all the other ingredients (except the cream) and bring to the boil.

Simmer for 20 minutes.

Blend the soup and stir in the vegan cream.

Gently reheat the soup and serve.

Serving suggestions

Warmed pitta bread triangles coated with vegan cheese, or vgf bread and cheese made into 'cheesy' toast.

Warm Red Pepper Soup

What you need

3 medium red onions finely chopped

4 medium red peppers finely chopped

1 can of chopped tomatoes

2 tbsp of vegan margarine

1 litre vgf stock

150ml vegan red wine

One handful of fresh parsley, chopped

One handful of fresh basil, chopped

1 tsp smoked paprika

½ tsp chilli flakes

What to do

Gently fry the onions and red peppers in the margarine for about 5 minutes until they are softened.

Add the paprika and chilli flakes and fry for a further 2-3 minutes.

Add the red wine and simmer for 3-4 minutes.

Add the vgf stock and tinned tomatoes, bring to the boil, and then simmer for 12-15 minutes.

Add the basil and parsley and simmer for a further 5 minutes.

Serving suggestions

Warmed vgf pitta bread triangles with melted vegan cheese, or warmed crusty vgf rolls.

Leek, Parsnip and Cashew Soup

What you need

2 medium sized leeks, finely chopped

3 medium sized parsnips, sliced

4 medium potatoes cut into small cubes

100g cashew nuts

1 tbsp rapeseed oil

750ml vgf stock

One handful of parsley, finely chopped

What to do

Gently fry the leeks in the rapeseed oil for about 5 minutes until they are softened.

Add the parsnips and potatoes and fry for a further 2 minutes, constantly stirring so the potatoes don't stick to the pan.

Add the stock, bring to the boil, and then simmer for 15 minutes.

Add the parsley and cashew nuts and simmer for a further 5 minutes.

Blend and serve – it makes a nice, thick soup!

Serving suggestions

Serve with potato wedges which have been coated in olive oil, turmeric and a sprinkle of chilli flakes and baked for 30 minutes – or perhaps with tortilla chips which have been baked so they're coated in melted vegan cheese.

Leek, parsnip and cashew soup served with turmeric and chilli potato wedges and tortilla chips with melted vegan cheese and herbs

Creamy Carrot and Coriander Soup

What you need

2 onions, finely chopped

8 medium-sized grated carrots

3 garlic cloves finely chopped

2.5cm cube fresh ginger, grated

250ml vegan cream

1 tbsp rapeseed oil

1 litre vgf stock

1 handful of chopped fresh coriander

What to do

Gently fry the onions in the rapeseed oil for about 5 minutes until they are softened.

Add the garlic and ginger and fry for 1-2 minutes, stirring constantly.

Add the carrots, vgf stock and coriander and bring to the boil. Simmer for 15-20 minutes.

Add the vegan cream and heat through for 4-5 minutes before blending.

Serving suggestions

With warmed vgf pitta bread triangles with melted vegan cheese, or with warmed vgf rolls.

Spicy Carrot and Orange Soup

What you need

2 onions, finely chopped

8 large carrots, diced

1 litre of vgf stock

The juice of two oranges

The grated zest of two oranges (half for the soup and half to garnish)

2 cloves of garlic, crushed

2.5cm cube of fresh ginger, grated

1 tbsp olive oil

2 tsp ground cumin

1 tsp turmeric

What to do

Fry the onions in olive oil until they are light brown.

Mix in the cumin, turmeric, garlic and ginger, and heat until it is like a paste, keep stirring well.

Add the carrots, vgf stock and orange juice.

Bring to the boil and then simmer for 20 minutes.

Stir in the zest from the second orange and blend the soup, reheating when needed.

Serving suggestions

Sprinkle linseeds, sunflower seeds and pumpkin seeds over the soup for a crunchy extra protein and omega boost. Serve with potato wedges.

Suppers

Polenta and Baby Tomatoes

What you need

A 500g packet of pre-prepared firm polenta cut into 1cm thick slices

About 30 baby tomatoes, quartered

50g of pitted black olives, sliced (or use pre-sliced ones for speed)

3 tbsp olive oil

4 cloves of garlic, crushed

One handful of mixed fresh herbs (basil, parsley, oregano), finely chopped

Salt and ground pepper to taste

What to do

Using a small amount of the olive oil, lightly oil a baking tray.

Arrange the sliced polenta side by side on the tray, until the tray is pretty well covered. Evenly arrange the tomatoes and olives over the sliced polenta.

Mix all the other ingredients together and drizzle the mixture over the tomatoes, adding salt and ground pepper to taste.

Bake in a preheated oven for 10-15 minutes at 200°C until the tomatoes are slightly browned and bubbling nicely.

Serving suggestions

Great on its own or with a side-salad, or serve with baked corn on the cob which has been drizzled with garlic-infused olive oil before baking.

Tortilla Chips, Salsa and Cucumber Dips

What you need

200g of tortilla chips

100g of vegan melting cheese, grated

For the dips:

Fresh Salsa

I crushed garlic clove

Half a chilli, finely chopped

30 baby tomatoes, finely chopped

1 handful of fresh, chopped basil

1 red onion, finely chopped

1 dstsp agave nectar

Cucumber dip

20cm of cucumber, cut into small cubes

1 handful of fresh coriander, mint, and parsley, finely chopped

3-4 mint leaves, finely chopped

4 spring onions, finely chopped

3 garlic cloves, crushed

250ml of vegan yogurt

What to do

Very finely chop the ingredients for each dip (except the vegan yogurt for the cucumber dip – add this once everything else is ready in the bowl) and place them in their separate bowls.

Add the yogurt to the cucumber dip.

Thoroughly mix both dips and place them in separate serving bowls.

Store both dips in the refrigerator until ready to serve.

Arrange the tortilla chips on two baking trays and sprinkle with grated vegan cheese.

Bake the tortilla chips for about 5 minutes at 200ºC, until the tortilla chips are lightly-browned and the vegan cheese melted.

Serve while hot with a spoonful each of the salsa and the cucumber and onion dips.

Serving suggestions

Serve with 'Traffic Light Chilli', another chilli, or a beany salad for a hearty main meal.

Traffic Light Sweet Chilli

What you need

3 peppers (one each of red, orange and green) sliced and chopped

2 400g(ish) cans of beans (e.g. adzuki, black-eyed, chickpeas, kidney, lentils) of your choice – drained

1 can of chopped tomatoes

1 tbsp rapeseed or olive oil

3-4 cloves of crushed garlic

1 tbsp maple syrup

1 tsp of chilli flakes or ½-1 chilli (depending on your level of bravery). We're not that brave, so if you like spicy, double up!

1 tsp turmeric

1 tsp ground cinnamon

What to do

Gently fry the chopped peppers in the oil until they're softened.

Add the chilli, garlic, cinnamon and turmeric and keep on stirring so the peppers don't stick to the pan.

Add the tomatoes, beans and maple syrup, and stir well.

Place the lid on the pot and simmer the chilli gently for 20-25 minutes, stirring regularly and adding a little water if necessary to prevent it from sticking.

Serving suggestions

Serve with brown or white rice, quinoa or corn couscous, and a dollop of plain vegan yogurt.

Shiitake, Tofu and Sesame Risotto

What you need

200g brown rice, washed

250g tofu cut into 1cm cubes

2 medium courgettes cut into 1cm cubes

10 shiitake mushrooms halved and sliced

10 chestnut mushrooms halved and sliced

1 red onion, finely chopped

750ml vgf stock

2 tbsp sesame oil

1 tbsp soy sauce

2 tsp dried oregano and 1 tsp of dried coriander

1 tsp ground cumin and 2 tsp of garlic granules

Sesame seeds to sprinkle on the tofu

What to do

Make up the vgf stock and add the oregano, coriander, cumin and garlic to the liquid. Put to one side.

Meanwhile, fry the onion in the rapeseed oil for 4-5 minutes until softened. Add the mushrooms and fry for another 4-5 minutes.

Add the washed brown rice and vgf stock mixture to the onions and mushrooms, cover and simmer for about 20-25 minutes.

Meanwhile, place the courgette and tofu on a baking tray and drizzle with sesame oil – bake for 10 minutes, checking them half-way through to turn them and make sure they are not sticking to the tray – if so, drizzle some more sesame oil onto them.

Drizzle the tofu with soy sauce and sprinkle with sesame seeds, and leave in the oven for a couple more minutes.

Remove the tofu from the oven and mix in with the mushroom and rice.

If there's still fluid in the rice mixture, simmer for another couple of minutes and then serve.

Serving suggestions

A baked potato and a fresh green salad.

Creamy Cashew Curly Kale

What you need

3 big handfuls of curly kale, finely sliced

2 medium onions, chopped

150g cashew nuts

15-20 olives, sliced

4 sundried tomatoes, chopped

6 artichoke pieces (from a jar), chopped

250ml carton of vegan cream

100ml of water

100ml white wine

1 tbsp olive oil

½ tsp of mustard of your choice

½ tsp of chilli flakes or a chopped chilli

What to do

Gently fry the onions in the olive oil for 4-5 minutes until softened.

Add the mustard and chilli and fry for a further 2-3 minutes. Add the wine and simmer for 3-4 minutes. Add the kale and water and reduce down with the lid on for about 10 minutes.

Add the sundried tomatoes, olives, artichokes, vegan cream and cashews and keep on the heat for about 10 minutes until well heated through and the kale is softened. Add a little more water if needed.

Serving Suggestions

Serve with brown rice, quinoa, or corn couscous.

Cashew and Sunflower Bake

What you need

6 carrots and 2 brown onions, grated

100g of cashew nuts and 50 g of sunflower seeds

2 vgf brown rolls made into breadcrumbs

100g of a strong vegan cheese, grated

500ml of vgf stock

Rapeseed oil to fry the onions and carrots and grease the loaf tin (with greaseproof paper)

2 tsp of dried mixed herbs

What to do

Fry the grated onions and carrots together in a little oil for 3-4 minutes. Transfer them to a mixing bowl.

In a food processor, make crumbs out of the two vgf rolls, the cashews, and sunflower seeds, and add to the mixing bowl.

Add the stock, herbs, and vegan cheese to the bowl, and mix well before placing in a suitable loaf tin that has been oiled and lined with greaseproof paper.

Bake covered with foil or a lid for 35-40 minutes at 210°C, and then another 10-15 minutes without the foil.

Serving suggestions

Great as part of a main celebratory meal with lots of side dishes and a homemade vgf onion gravy or vgf bread and onion sauce.

Spicy Sweetcorn Chickpea Patties

What you need

2 cans of chickpeas, drained and blended with 1 can of sweetcorn until smooth

6 spring onions, finely chopped

2 large carrots, grated

4 vgf brown rolls made into breadcrumbs

1 handful of fresh coriander, finely chopped

2 tsp of mild curry powder

4 garlic cloves, crushed

4 tbsp sunflower oil (for frying)

What to do

Gently fry the spring onions in a small amount of the sunflower oil, keeping the rest of the oil for frying the patties. Add the grated carrots, curry powder, and garlic and fry for another 1-2 minutes.

Place the spring onion and carrot mixture in a large mixing bowl and add the chickpeas, sweetcorn, breadcrumbs, and coriander.

Mix well, shape them into flat rounds and leave them in a fridge for a couple of hours. Add a little water if needed. Finally, gently fry the patties in the sunflower oil until they're crisp and golden brown on both sides.

Serving suggestions

Serve with a baked potato or on a vgf roll with a mixed salad and sliced tomato.

Quick Chickpea Pea Curry

What you need

2 onions, finely chopped

1 red pepper, finely chopped

1 green pepper, finely chopped

2 carrots, grated

2 handfuls of spinach chopped

1 can of chopped tomatoes

2 cans of chickpeas, drained

1 can of sweetcorn, drained

100g frozen peas

1 tbsp olive oil

2-3 tsp curry powder (depending on taste)

500ml vgf stock

What to do

Lightly fry the onions and peppers for 4-5 minutes in olive oil.

Add the curry powder and mix thoroughly, frying for 2-3 minutes.

Add the grated carrots, spinach, chopped tomatoes, peas, sweetcorn, can of chickpeas, and vgf stock.

Simmer the curry for 20 minutes.

Serving Suggestions

Serve with white rice, wild rice, brown rice, quinoa, or corn couscous.

Vegan Bean Sauspot

What you need

8 vgf sausages, cooked and cut into 1cm slices

1 red onion, quartered and sliced

1 brown onion, quartered and sliced

2 sliced courgettes

1 can of black-eyed beans, drained

1 can of borlotti beans, drained

1 can of chopped tomatoes

4 sundried tomatoes finely chopped

1 tbsp rapeseed oil

200ml vegan red wine

1 tsp Dijon mustard

1 handful of fresh parsley, chopped

1 red chilli finely chopped

1 tbsp unrefined sugar or agave nectar (optional)

What to do

Cook the vgf sausages and put them to one side.

Meanwhile, gently fry the onions in the rapeseed oil for 4-5 minutes. Add the wine and mustard and simmer for 3-4 minutes.

Add all the other ingredients and simmer for 10-12 minutes. Slice the cooked vgf sausages into 1cm slices and stir them into the casserole.

Simmer for 3-4 more minutes and serve.

Serving Suggestions

Sprinkle with nutritional flakes or grated vegan cheese, and serve with vgf garlic bread.

Nutty Mushroom Burgers

What you need

200g button mushrooms, finely chopped

2 garlic cloves

100g chopped hazelnuts

100g pecan nuts, chopped

1 red onion, finely chopped

4 slices vgf bread made into breadcrumbs

1 tbsp nutritional yeast

1 tbsp of tomato puree

100ml of hot boiled water mixed with 1 tsp of yeast extract

2 tbsp of sunflower oil

1 handful of fresh parsley, chopped

What to do

Gently fry the red onion in a small amount of the sunflower oil for 3-4 minutes. Add the chopped mushrooms and garlic and stir for 2 minutes, while keeping the pan on the heat. Meanwhile, mix the yeast extract in the hot water.

In a mixing bowl add the mushroom mixture to all the other ingredients (except the remaining oil) and mix thoroughly.

Make into burger shapes, adding more vgf breadcrumbs or more water depending on whether too wet/dry. Put to cool in the fridge for an hour. Finally, shallow fry them until they are browned on each side.

Serving Suggestions

Serve in chunky vgf rolls with vgf mayonnaise and sliced tomatoes and/or sliced gherkins.

Dhal

What you need

200g of dried red lentils

2 medium onions, chopped

10 baby tomatoes, halved

600ml of water

1 tbsp rapeseed oil

1 red chilli (or half if you prefer mild dhal) finely chopped

4 garlic cloves, chopped and mixed with 3cm cube of grated ginger

1 tbsp tomato puree

1 tsp salt

1 tsp mustard seeds

1 tsp cumin seeds

1 tsp turmeric

A handful of chopped coriander

What to do

Gently fry the onions, chilli, mustard seeds, turmeric and cumin seeds in the rapeseed oil for 4-5 minutes. Add the garlic and ginger paste and fry for another 1-2 minutes, constantly stirring.

Add the tomatoes, lentils, water and tomato puree and simmer for 20-25 minutes, until the tomatoes are soft and the lentils cooked.

Add the chopped coriander and simmer the dhal for 2-3 minutes before serving.

Serving Suggestions

Serve with vegan yogurt, rice and/or vgf pitta bread. For a big, spicy, shared meal, serve with vegetable biryani and aubergine and lentil curry.

Vegetable Biryani

What you need

2 onions, chopped

200g of basmati rice, well rinsed

2 carrots, scrubbed and sliced

2 medium potatoes, finely cubed

Handful of green beans, chopped

200g cashew nuts

4 garlic cloves, chopped and mixed with 3cm cube of grated ginger

1 litre of water

½ tsp salt

1 green chilli, chopped

3 bay leaves

5 cardamom pods

1 tsp chilli powder

1 tsp curry powder

What to do

In a deep pan, fry the onions and chillies until the onions are browned and the chillies softened.

Add the remaining ingredients (except the cashew nuts), mix well, cover with the lid, and simmer for 18-20 minutes, stirring regularly. Add the cashew nuts for the last few minutes of cooking

Remove the cardamom pods and bay leaves before serving

Serving Suggestions

Serve with dhal (on previous page) and vgf pitta and/or a side salad.

Sundried Tomato Pasta

What you need

200g vgf pasta of your choice

2 onions, finely chopped

1 can of chopped tomatoes

8 sundried tomatoes, chopped

4 cloves of garlic, crushed

100g vegan cheese, grated

150ml vegan red wine

1 tbsp of olive oil

2 tbsp of tomato puree

1 tsp of paprika

A handful of fresh parsley, a handful of fresh basil and a few sprigs of oregano, chopped

What to do

Gently fry the onions in the olive oil for 3-4 minutes. Add the garlic and fry for a further 1-2 minutes. Add all the remaining ingredients (except the pasta) and simmer for 10-15 minutes.

While the tomato mixture is simmering, cook the pasta. Once both are cooked, mix the tomato sauce with the pasta and serve.

Serving suggestions

Sprinkle with vegan parmesan or yeast flakes.

Nutty Vegetable Crumble

What you need

5 medium sized carrots sliced or cubed

2 medium sized leeks, sliced

2 courgettes, sliced

1 small swede, cubed

1 medium sweet potato, cubed

1 tsp mustard

750ml vgf stock

A pinch of pepper

For the crumble

250g brown gluten free flour

50g vegan margarine

100g chopped nuts

1 tsp mustard

100g vegan cheese, grated

2 tsp dried mixed herbs

Salt and pepper as required

What to do

In a large saucepan, gently fry the sliced leeks in rapeseed oil and then add all of the remaining vegetables to the pan.

Add the vgf stock and mustard and bring to the boil, leaving to simmer for 10-15 minutes.

Meanwhile, place all of the crumble ingredients in a mixing bowl and rub them between your fingers to create the nutty crumble.

Once the vegetables have simmered, transfer them to a casserole dish and top with the crumble mix.

Bake the crumble covered with foil or a suitable lid at 210 degrees Centigrade for 20-30 minutes, and then without the lid for 10-15 minutes until browned.

Serving Suggestions

Serve with potato wedges and broccoli and/or asparagus.

Nutty vegetable crumble

Spicy Soya Mince Fajitas

What you need

1 tbsp of olive oil

2 onions, finely chopped

1 mug vgf soya mince, hydrated as per the instructions on the packet (with vgf stock)

1 can of chopped tomatoes

3 cloves of garlic, crushed

1 tbsp tomato puree

1 tsp chilli powder or chilli flakes mixed with 2 tsp ground cumin, 2 tsp smoked paprika

2 tsp oregano

8 tortillas, warmed just before serving

What to do

Fry the onions in olive oil for 4-5 minutes until softened and light brown. Add the garlic, cumin, chilli and paprika and fry for a further 1-2 minutes, stirring to make sure it doesn't stick to the pan.

Add the hydrated mince, tomatoes, oregano and tomato puree and simmer the mixture for 15 minutes.

When the soya mixture is ready to serve, spoon the mixture onto the warmed tortillas.

Serving suggestions

Serve with vegan yogurt and an onion/cucumber/baby tomato salad.

Ginger and Orange Chunks

What you need

400g firm tofu, cut into 1.5cm cubes

2 medium/large carrots, grated

1 large onion, finely chopped

200ml fresh orange juice

2.5cm piece of ginger, grated and mixed with 4 cloves of crushed garlic

2 tbsp sesame oil

2 tbsp sunflower oil

2 tbsp vgf soy sauce

What to do

Mix the orange juice, garlic, ginger and soy sauce together in a bowl and marinate the tofu chunks for 20 minutes. Meanwhile, fry the onions for 4-5 minutes in the sunflower oil. Add the grated carrot and stir-fry for a further 3-4 minutes.

Remove the tofu cubes from the marinade and gently fry them in another pan with the sesame oil until they are lightly browned. Add the carrots and onions to the remaining marinade and mix well. When the tofu is light brown on both sides, add the carrot and onion marinade mixture to the pan and simmer for 10 minutes.

Serving suggestions

Serve with vgf noodles or rice.

Baked Aubergine in Mushroom Sauce

What you need

2 medium-sized aubergines (eggplants), cut into ¾ cm slices

½ tsp salt

1 tbsp olive oil

2 tsp lemon juice

For the sauce:

200g of button mushrooms, thinly sliced

1 carton of vegan cream

100ml white wine

1 tbsp vegan margarine

1 handful of chopped parsley

What to do

Slice the aubergines and wash them thoroughly in a colander under running water.

Arrange them on a grill tray, brush them with olive oil and sprinkle them with salt and lemon juice.

Once browned on one side, turn them over and repeat the procedure on the other side.

Meanwhile, melt the margarine in a saucepan and add the mushrooms – fry for 4-5 minutes.

Add the garlic to the mushrooms and stir for

1-2 minutes.

Add the wine and simmer for 3-4 minutes

Stir in the cream and parsley and simmer for a further 4-5 minutes.

Remove the aubergine slices from the oven and arrange them on serving plates.

Pour the mushroom sauce over the aubergines.

Serving suggestions

Serve with potato wedges.

Baked aubergine in mushroom sauce

Nutty Creamy Cauliflower

What you need

1 large cauliflower cut into florets

1 leek, finely chopped

150g of button mushrooms, sliced

2 tbsp each of chopped hazelnuts and flaked almonds

100g vegan cheese, grated

1 tbsp of sunflower oil

100ml soya or rice milk

200ml soya or rice cream

1 handful of fresh flat parsley, chopped

2 tsp Dijon mustard

Salt and pepper to taste

What to do

Boil or steam the chopped cauliflower for 8-10 minutes.

Meanwhile, in a frying pan gently fry the chopped leek and mushrooms for 3-4 minutes in sunflower oil. Add the soya milk, soya cream, mustard, nuts and parsley and simmer for 2-3 minutes until the sauce is smooth – do not boil but keep on stirring.

Drain the cauliflower and arrange it in an oven proof dish. Pour the sauce over the cauliflower and sprinkle the vegan cheese on top. Bake at 200°C for 15 minutes, until the top is golden brown and bubbling.

Serving Suggestions

Serve with vgf garlic bread and salad.

Creamy Tomato & Almond Vegetables

What you need

50g flaked almonds

A big handful of spinach, chopped

200g button mushrooms, halved

1 onion, chopped

2 courgettes, sliced

100g baby tomatoes, halved

3 garlic cloves, crushed

250ml vegan white wine

100ml vegan yogurt

250ml vegan cream

1 tbsp olive oil

A handful of parsley, chopped

What to do

Gently fry the onions in the olive oil for 4-5 minutes, and then add the mushrooms and courgettes and fry for a further 3-4 minutes, stirring regularly.

Add the wine and simmer for 3 minutes. Add the flaked almonds, fresh tomatoes, spinach, parsley, and garlic and simmer for 2-3 minutes.

Stir in the vegan yogurt and vegan cream and heat through, stirring regularly.

Serving Suggestions

Serve with a baked potato, vgf pasta or brown rice.

Quick Curried Butter Beans

What you need

2 cans of butter beans, half drained

1 yellow pepper finely chopped

1 green chilli finely chopped

1 large onion, chopped

4 cloves of garlic, crushed and blended with a 3cm piece of ginger, grated

2 tbsp rapeseed oil

2 tsp curry powder

What to do

Gently fry the onion, pepper and chilli in the rapeseed oil until they are softened.

Mix in the garlic/ginger paste and curry powder and stir fry for 1-2 minutes.

Add the tomatoes and butter beans and stir well, leaving to simmer for 10 minutes.

Serving suggestions

Serve with rice, vegan yogurt, vgf poppadoms and/or vgf pitta bread.

Easy Almond and Fennel Curry

What you need

1 fennel bulb, finely sliced

1 onion, sliced

10 baby sweetcorns, sliced lengthways

15-20 fine beans, chopped

10 mushrooms, sliced

4 large very ripe tomatoes, quartered

4 handfuls of spring greens

50g flaked almonds

1 tbsp olive oil

2 tsp mild curry powder

1 tsp garam masala

1 tsp ground ginger

What to do

Fry all of the ingredients in the olive oil for 15 minutes (except for the spices and flaked almonds), stirring regularly. Add the spices and stir for a couple more minutes.

Add the flaked almonds and keep the pan on the heat for 5 minutes, removing the lid and stirring 3-4 times to make sure nothing is sticking to the pan (it's quite a dry curry).

Serving suggestions

Serve with brown rice for a good, hearty meal.

Green and Yellow Creamy Nutty Curry

What you need

2 small, or one medium, onion (s), sliced

1 head of broccoli, chopped into halved florets

2-3 yellow or green courgettes, sliced

1 green or yellow pepper, thinly sliced

150g cashew nuts

50g pine nuts

1 can of coconut milk

1 tbsp sunflower or rapeseed oil

200ml water

2.5 cm of fresh ginger, grated and mixed with 1 chopped chilli, 4 crushed garlic cloves, 1 tsp turmeric, and 1 tsp ground cinnamon

What to do

Gently fry the onions and peppers in the sunflower oil with the ginger, chilli, garlic, turmeric and cinnamon.

Add the broccoli, courgettes and water. Stir well, bring to the boil, and then simmer for 12-15 minutes (until broccoli almost cooked). Add the coconut milk and nuts and simmer for another 5 minutes.

Serving Suggestions

Serve with quinoa or rice and some vgf poppadoms.

Pine Nut and Sweetcorn Risotto

What you need

1 onion, chopped	50g pine nuts
6-8 spring onions, chopped	100g vegan cheese, grated (or use nutritional yeast flakes)
2 peppers, chopped	
Handful of rocket, shredded	200g rice, rinsed
Handful of spinach, shredded	500ml vgf stock
	125ml rice milk
Chopped mushrooms	1 tbsp of chilli and garlic-infused olive oil
1 can of sweetcorn	

What to do

Stir-fry the onions, spring onions, peppers, and mushrooms in the chilli/garlic olive oil for 4-5 minutes. Add the pine nuts and stir-fry for another 2-3 minutes.

Add the rice, water, spinach, sweetcorn, rocket and vgf stock and simmer until most of the water is absorbed. Add the rice milk and keep on stirring for 3-4 minutes.

Sprinkle with grated vegan cheese once served (or nutritional yeast flakes if you prefer).

Serving suggestions

Serve as a main or a side dish with roasted mixed vegetables.

VGF All Day Breakfast

What you need

For the tofu scramble:

A block of tofu, mashed and mixed with:

1 red onion, chopped and fried in a little oil

1 tsp of onion powder mixed with ½ tsp of turmeric, ½ tsp of paprika, 1 tsp of oregano

For the rest of the breakfast:

Mushrooms, fried in a little vegan spread

Tomatoes, halved and baked

Baby potatoes, baked

Vgf sausages, fried or baked

What to do

If having baby potatoes, drizzle them with a little olive oil and place in the oven to bake. After 10 minutes, put the tomatoes and vgf sausages in the oven too.

Meanwhile, fry the mushrooms in the vegan margarine, and in a separate pan, fry the red onion until softened and then add the mashed tofu. Keep stirring the tofu and after a few minutes add the onion powder, turmeric, paprika and oregano – keep stirring.

Serving suggestions

With vgf toast and baked beans. This is something we have on one of those days when we've been working hard at work or in the garden and are lacking inspiration.

Tofu Italia

What you need

2 brown onions, chopped

1 aubergine, cubed

2 courgettes, sliced

1 red pepper, thinly sliced

100g baby plum tomatoes, halved

50g black pitted olives

50g preserved artichokes

1 block of tofu halved lengthways and cut into ½ cm thickness pieces

1 tbsp rapeseed oil for frying and 2 tbsp garlic-infused olive oil for the roasted vegetables.

2 tbsp vgf soy sauce

2 tsp dried oregano

1 tbsp agave nectar

What to do

Place the onions, aubergine, courgettes, pepper and tomatoes on a baking tray. Drizzle with garlic-infused oil and bake for 15-20 minutes, regularly turning the vegetables. Add the olives and sliced artichokes and bake for another 4-5 minutes.

Pan-fry the tofu until browned on both sides. Add the vgf soy sauce mixed with the oregano and agave nectar, and coat the tofu on both sides. Serve with the roasted vegetables.

Serving suggestions

Serve with brown rice pasta. Sprinkle with yeast flakes or grated vegan cheese.

Tofu Scramble and Spinach on Toast

What you need

1 block of silken tofu, mashed

1 onion, finely chopped

2 big handfuls of spinach, shredded

1 tbsp vegan gluten free soy sauce

50ml rice milk

1 tbsp rapeseed oil

½ tsp turmeric

1 tsp oregano

2 heaped tsp onion granules

4 vgf bread rolls of your choice, halved and toasted

What to do

Gently fry the chopped onion in the rapeseed oil for 4-5 minutes. Add the spinach and cover the pan, frequently removing the lid to stir.

Meanwhile, mix the mashed tofu, turmeric, oregano and onion granules together in a bowl.

Add the tofu mixture to the onions and now-wilted spinach, and keep on stirring until heated through. Add the rice milk and keep on stirring for 2-3 minutes.

Serving suggestions

Serve on top of the halved vgf toasted rolls.

Rich Red Wine Lentil Casserole

What you need

2 large red onions, chopped

200g mushrooms, sliced

1 broccoli head, chopped

A bunch (about 15-20) of fine asparagus, chopped into 3cm pieces

2 carrots, sliced

1 can green lentils, drained

200ml red wine

Handful of fresh oregano, parsley, and basil, chopped

1 tsp yeast extract mixed with 1 tbsp tomato puree, 2 dstsp agave nectar, and 500ml recently boiled hot water

What to do

Prepare the yeast extract/tomato puree gravy and put to one side.

Meanwhile, fry the onions and mushrooms in a little oil for about 4-5 minutes. Add the wine and simmer for 3-4 minutes.

Add the remaining ingredients, bring to the boil and then simmer for 20 minutes.

Serving suggestions

A lovely, rich casserole. Great served with a vgf pizza base, which has been baked coated in olive oil and a little garlic salt and a sprinkling of grated vegan cheese.

Lentil Chilli Corn Couscous

What you need

175g of maize couscous made up as per instructions on the packet and left to one side

2 brown onions, chopped

1 green pepper chopped

1 leek, chopped

8 spring onions, chopped

1 can of borlotti beans, drained

1 can of lentils, drained

1 can of chopped tomatoes

1 small can of chopped pineapple

1 tbsp tomato puree

1 tbsp rapeseed oil

4 garlic cloves, crushed

1 tsp chilli flakes

1 tsp ground turmeric

2.5cm of ginger, grated

1 tsp of mixed herbs

What to do

Gently fry the chopped onions, spring onions, leek and pepper in the rapeseed oil for 4-5 minutes. Add the garlic, chilli, turmeric and ginger and stir for 4-5 minutes. Add the lentils, borlotti beans, pineapple, tomato puree, herbs and tomatoes, cover the pan and simmer for 10 minutes, removing the lid frequently to stir.

Once cooked, stir the vegetables into the cooked maize couscous and keep on the heat for 2-3 minutes, stirring thoroughly.

Serving Suggestions

Serve with a baked potato and a green salad with chopped grapes.

Walnut Gluten Free Penne

What you need

150g vgf penne, cooked as per the packet

2 large onions, finely chopped

20 baby mushrooms, sliced

100g broken walnuts

1 can of chopped tomatoes

1 tbsp tomato puree

100ml vegan cream

1 tbsp agave nectar

1 tbsp rapeseed oil

1 red chilli chopped

A handful of fresh, finely-chopped coriander and parsley

What to do

Gently fry the onions, mushrooms, and chilli in a little rapeseed oil for 3-4 minutes.

Add the walnuts, tomatoes, and tomato puree, and simmer for 8-10 minutes.

Mix in the vegan cream, agave nectar, coriander and parsley and simmer for another 5 minutes, stirring regularly.

Serving suggestions

Serve with vgf garlic bread and a dollop of vegan yogurt.

Mushroom Dry Curry

What you need

12-15 cherry tomatoes, halved

200g button mushrooms, halved

2 medium potatoes, chopped into small 2cm chunks

1 large onion, chopped

1 red chilli, chopped

3 cloves of garlic, crushed

2 tbsp rapeseed oil

1 tsp cinnamon

1 tsp cumin

1 tbsp curry powder

Handful of fresh coriander, chopped

What to do

Gently fry the onion and chilli for 3-4 minutes in the rapeseed oil.

Add the cubed potatoes, button mushrooms and garlic, and continue to fry for 3-4 minutes, constantly stirring to prevent the vegetables from sticking to the pan.

Add the cinnamon, cumin, curry powder and coriander and stir thoroughly for 1-2 minutes.

Stir in the chopped tomatoes and coriander and simmer for 20-25 minutes until the potatoes are softened.

Serving Suggestions

Serve with poppadoms and brown or basmati rice, and a side onion salad of onion, chopped baby tomatoes, and chopped coriander and mint.

Roasted Vegetable Nut Roast

What you need

50g pine nuts

100g pecan nuts

100g cashew nuts

50g sunflower seeds

2 red peppers, sliced

2 red onions, sliced

100g mushrooms, sliced

3 courgettes, sliced

1 tin of green lentils, drained

4 vgf brown rolls made into bread crumbs

1 tbsp tomato puree

2 tbsp olive oil mixed with 4 cloves of crushed garlic

A handful of fresh, mixed herbs, chopped (I used parsley, oregano and marjoram)

300ml vgf stock

What to do

Arrange the peppers, onions, courgettes and mushrooms on a baking tray and drizzle with the olive oil and garlic mixture. Roast in the oven at 200°C for 15-20 minutes, carefully turning the vegetables over several times, making sure they don't burn.

Meanwhile, chop the nuts and herbs (in a food processor) and place them in a mixing bowl with the breadcrumbs, lentils, tomato puree and vgf stock.

Once the vegetables are cooked, mix them in with the bread and nut mixture.

Press the mixture into an ovenproof, greased and/or lined baking dish, and blind bake covered with a lid or foil for 20 minutes, and then uncovered for a further 20 minutes.

Serving Suggestions   Serve with salad and vgf garlic bread, but this is also a great Christmas/special celebration nut roast, so the usual potatoes, vgf gravy, cranberry sauce, and lots and lots of sprouts, are all great accompaniments. We have it EVERY Christmas!

Pesto Pasta

What you need

200g vgf pasta of your choice

2 tbsp olive oil

50g pine nuts

Half a garlic bulb (about 5 cloves) peeled

A large handful of basil leaves

50g vegan cheese, grated

What to do   Put the pasta on to cook as per the instructions on the packet.

Blend all the other ingredients in a food processor until it makes a nice, grainy sauce.

Once the pasta is cooked and drained (rinse it if necessary), coat the pasta with the pesto sauce before serving. Serve nice and hot.

Serving suggestions   This is such a quick meal. Serve with a side of baked Portobello mushrooms and a side salad. Also great with nutritional yeast flakes on the top or added to the sauce.

Chunky Stew

What you need

2 onions, sliced

200g soya chunks, hydrated as indicated on the packet

3 medium carrots, sliced

3 medium parsnips, sliced

2 medium courgettes, sliced

1 tbsp tomato puree

150ml white wine

750ml vgf stock

2 tsp yeast extract

Handful of fresh mixed herbs (parsley, sage, rosemary, thyme and oregano), chopped

What to do

Lightly fry the onions for 3-4 minutes.

Add the white wine, carrots and parsnips and continue to fry for 3-4 minutes.

Add the yeast extract, vgf stock and tomato puree, and simmer for 4-5 minutes.

Add the soya chunks and courgettes and simmer for 15 minutes, stirring occasionally.

Serving suggestions

Serve with mashed potatoes and broccoli stems.

Lightly Battered Tofu

What you need

2 blocks of tofu, drained and chopped into 1cm slices

50g plain vgf flour to coat the tofu

2 tbsp sesame seeds

100ml vegan white wine

2 tbsp vgf soy sauce

1 tbsp of agave nectar

Sunflower oil for frying

What to do

Make a batter by mixing together the vgf flour, vegan wine, soy sauce, agave nectar and sesame seeds.

Coat the tofu slices in the batter.

Heat the sunflower oil in a deep frying pan and fry the coated tofu slices.

When nicely browned, turn the tofu slices over to coat the other sides.

As you make them, put them under a grill on a low heat to keep them warm, while you repeat with the rest of the tofu slices.

Serving suggestions

Serve on a bed of rice with a side salad and a dash of vgf chilli sauce.

Tofu Chow Mein

What you need

400g block of firm tofu, cut into 2cm cubes	2 packets of rice noodles
2 onions, sliced	50 g sesame seeds
15-20 baby sweetcorns	½ tsp chilli flakes
20 mangetout	Sesame oil for frying
1 tin of bamboo shoots, drained (optional)	2 tbsp soy sauce
100g fresh bean sprouts	

What to do

Fry the tofu cubes in half of the sesame oil. Pour on the soy sauce and, once the tofu is nicely browned, put them to one side to keep them warm.

Stir-fry the onions, baby sweetcorns, mangetout, chilli and bamboo shoots for 4-5 minutes.

Add the noodles and bean sprouts and continue to stir-fry until the noodles are soft, adding extra soy sauce and a little water if required. Toss in the tofu cubes and serve with the sesame seeds sprinkled over the top.

Serving suggestions

Serve with a mixed green salad.

Sweet and Sour Tofu

What you need

400g block of firm tofu, cubed and marinated in vgf soy sauce

15-20 baby sweetcorns

2 onions, sliced

1 orange pepper, sliced

1 red pepper, sliced

15-20 button mushrooms

15 baby tomatoes, washed and left whole

20 fine green beans

4 slices of tinned pineapple, pureed

1 chilli, chopped

1 tbsp tomato puree

1 tbsp sesame oil

1 tbsp agave nectar

1 tbsp lemon juice

What to do

Place the marinated tofu on an oiled baking tray and bake for 10-15 minutes, turning the cubes often until they're nicely browned.

Gently fry the onion and peppers in the sesame oil for 3-4 minutes. Add the chilli, sweetcorn, green beans, and button mushrooms and fry for a further 3-4 minutes.

Add the baby tomatoes and the tomato puree, agave nectar, lemon juice and pineapple puree and simmer for 12-15 minutes, adding the tofu cubes for the final few minutes.

Serving suggestions

Serve with rice or vgf noodles.

Adzuki Bean Stew

What you need

2 cans of adzuki beans, drained and washed

2 onions, chopped

Handful of spinach, chopped

20 baby tomatoes, left whole

1 tin of chopped tomatoes

500ml vgf stock

1 tbsp sunflower oil

1 tbsp tomato puree

3 cloves garlic, chopped

Handful of chopped fresh herbs – coriander, parsley and oregano

What to do

Gently fry the onion in sunflower oil for 3-4 minutes.

Add the garlic, tomato puree and baby tomatoes and stir-fry for a further 2-3 minutes.

Add the spinach, beans, tinned tomatoes, vgf stock and herbs and simmer for 10-15 minutes.

Serving suggestions

Serve with rice, a baked potato, or vgf bread rolls with melted vegan cheese on them.

Vegan Sausage Ratatouille

What you need

8 vgf sausages	3 garlic cloves, sliced
1 aubergine, cubed	2 tbsp olive oil
3 medium courgettes, sliced	500ml of vgf stock
	1 tbsp agave nectar
1 red pepper, chopped	1 tbsp tomato puree
2 large red onions, sliced	2 tsp dried oregano
	1 tsp dried thyme
1 tin of chopped tomatoes	

What to do

Cook the vgf sausages as per the instructions on the packet and, once they are cool enough, cut them into 1cm slices.

Gently fry the onions, peppers and aubergine for 3-4 minutes in olive oil.

Add the garlic and fry for a further 1-2 minutes.

Add the remaining ingredients, bring to the boil, and then simmer for 15 minutes.

Add the sausages and simmer for a further 5 minutes.

Serving suggestions

Serve with salad and vgf rolls or baked potatoes.

Falafels and Salsa

What you need

2 x 400g tins of chickpeas, drained

1 handful of fresh parsley, chopped

2 onions, finely chopped

3 cloves of garlic, crushed

Vgf pitta breads or wraps of your choice

2 tsp of ground cumin

2 tsp of ground coriander

1 tsp of medium curry powder

5 slices of brown vgf bread (or 7-8 small slices) made into breadcrumbs

2 tbsp of sunflower/rapeseed oil

What to do

Gently fry the onions in sunflower oil for 4-5 minutes until they are softened. Add the garlic and fry for a further 1-2 minutes.

Blend the chickpeas in a food processor until they are smooth. Place the chickpeas with the onions and all the other ingredients in a bowl and mix thoroughly.

Shape the mixture into 12-16 round balls and leave to one side for half an hour.

Bake in an oven on an oiled tray at 180 degrees centigrade for 30-35 minutes until nicely browned (turn them half way through).

Serving suggestions

Serve in salad-stuffed vgf pitta breads drizzled with salsa and a cucumber dip (both pages 39-40)

Spinach Lasagne

What you need

For the filling:

10 asparagus tips, chopped into 2cm pieces

1 pepper, sliced

2 onions, sliced

2 courgettes, sliced

100g mushrooms, sliced

1 tin of chopped tomatoes

1 tbsp of agave nectar

Vgf lasagne sheets – about 10-12 pieces

500 ml vgf stock

For the spinach sauce:

100ml rice milk

100ml vegan cream

Handful of spinach

3 garlic cloves, crushed

Handful of fresh parsley, chopped

3-4 sprigs of fresh oregano, chopped

100g vegan cheese, grated

What to do

Place the asparagus, pepper, onions, courgettes and mushrooms on a baking tray, drizzle with olive oil and bake for 15 minutes at 200°C, turning the vegetables over halfway through. Roast until they are light brown on both sides and put them to one side.

Place them in a pan with the canned tomatoes and the vgf stock and simmer for 5-6 minutes.

In a food mixer blend the spinach sauce

ingredients together.

Arrange half of the roast vegetables in the bottom of an ovenproof dish.

Cover with a layer of the vgf lasagne, followed by a layer of tomatoes, and then a further layer of lasagne, followed by another layer of vegetables.

Finally, add a layer of lasagne, and cover with the vegan cheese and spinach sauce.

Bake for 25-30 minutes at 200°C (covered for first 10-15 minutes).

Serving suggestions

Serve with vgf garlic bread, salad and/or potato wedges

Lentil, Tomato and Mushroom Risotto

What you need

200g rice, washed

100g red lentils, washed

1 large onion, chopped

100g cherry tomatoes, halved

100g mushrooms, sliced

4 cloves of garlic, crushed 1 tbsp of olive oil

750ml vgf stock

1 handful of fresh parsley, chopped

A few sprigs of oregano, chopped

What to do

Gently fry the onions for 2-3 minutes in the olive oil.

Add the mushrooms and garlic and stir fry for a further 2-3 minutes, then add the tomatoes, rice and lentils and stir well.

Add the vgf stock, simmer, and continue to stir frequently to prevent the rice or lentils from sticking.

After 10 minutes, add the parsley and oregano and continue to stir frequently until the rice and lentils are soft.

Serving suggestions

Serve with vgf rolls, or 'cheesy' vgf pittas and salad or side vegetables.

Apricot and Sweet Potato Curry

What you need

2 medium sweet potatoes, peeled and cut into 1cm cubes

2 medium onions, sliced

2 courgettes, sliced

100g dried (orange) apricots, quartered

3 garlic cloves, crushed and blended with 3cm piece of fresh ginger, grated

1 red chilli, chopped

1 tbsp rapeseed oil

500 ml vgf stock

Handful of fresh, chopped coriander

½ tsp cumin

1 tsp turmeric

What to do

Gently fry the onions and chilli in rapeseed oil for 4-5 minutes.

Add the cubes of sweet potato, apricots, courgettes, garlic/ginger paste, cumin, coriander and turmeric, and stir-fry for 2 minutes.

Cover with vgf stock to the top of the sweet potatoes and apricots, and simmer for 15 minutes.

Serving suggestions

Serve with brown or basmati rice and poppadoms, or vgf pitta bread triangles and/or potato wedges.

Vegan Burgers in a Mushroom Sauce

What you need

For the burgers:

2 mugs of soya mince hydrated with one mug of vgf stock

1 handful of fresh chopped parsley and oregano

2 onions, finely chopped

4 vgf brown rolls made into breadcrumbs

4 tbsp vgf self raising flour

500ml of vgf stock

Sunflower oil (for frying the burgers)

For the sauce:

300g mushrooms, finely chopped

4 cloves of garlic, crushed

2 tbsp tomato puree

2 tbsp vegan margarine

200ml vegan cream

1 small handful of fresh coriander, chopped

1 handful of fresh parsley, chopped

What to do

In a food mixer blend together the burger ingredients (except the sunflower oil) and shape the mixture into flat burger shapes – dust them with plain vgf flour and put them to one side for 20 minutes.

Meanwhile, gently fry the chopped mushrooms in vegan margarine for 5-6 minutes. Add the garlic and continue to fry for 1-2 minutes. Add the parsley, coriander, and vegan cream and simmer for about 5 minutes, stirring regularly – put the sauce to one side to keep it warm.

Gently fry the veggie burgers in the sunflower oil until they are light brown and crispy on both sides.

Pour the mushroom sauce over the burgers.

Serving suggestions

Serve with salad and baked potatoes or potato wedges.

Vegan burgers in a mushroom sauce

Summer Vegetable Wraps

What you need

2 courgettes, quartered lengthways and cut into 3 cm sticks

4 spring onions, chopped into 3cm long sticks

4 carrots, cut into 3 cm long sticks

200g mushrooms, sliced

2 peppers of your choice cut into sticks

1 tbsp olive oil

Handful of spinach, shredded

4 cloves of garlic, crushed

1 tsp smoked paprika

What to do

Gently stir-fry the carrots, mushrooms, onions, peppers and courgettes in olive oil for 7-8 minutes. Add the crushed garlic and fry for a further 2-3 minutes.

Add the spinach, tomato puree and paprika and simmer for 4-5 minutes.

Serving suggestions

This is inspired by a trip many years ago to Matlock in Derbyshire. Serve in rolled, warmed vgf wraps with vegan yogurt (or houmous), salsa and a side salad, or you could add marinated, pan-fried tofu or chopped nuts for an extra protein fix. If you have more time it is worth roasting the vegetables instead.

Pepper, Peach and Olive Quinoa

What you need

3 peppers (One each of red, orange, and yellow), chopped

4 spring onions, chopped

12-15 baby tomatoes, left whole

20 pitted olives, sliced

1 can of sliced peaches, chopped

50g of pine nuts

1 tbsp olive oil

250g of quinoa, washed and cooked as per the direction on the packet

What to do

Cook the washed quinoa as directed, stirring regularly.

Meanwhile, in a separate pan, gently fry the peppers and spring onions in the olive oil for 5-6 minutes.

Add the baby tomatoes and olives and fry for a further 3-4 minutes.

Add the quinoa, pine nuts and peach pieces and toss until evenly distributed.

Serving suggestions

Serve with vgf garlic bread and/or a salad.

Banana and Mushroom Curry

What you need

1 ripe banana, mashed

300g of mushrooms, sliced

2 onions, chopped

1 tbsp of rapeseed oil

2.5cm piece of ginger grated and blended with 4 cloves garlic

1 tbsp of tomato puree

1 can of coconut milk

½-1 chilli, chopped

1 tsp cumin seeds

1 tsp mustard seeds

1 tsp cinnamon

2 tsp curry powder

What to do

Gently fry the onions and chilli in a pan for 4-5 minutes.

Add the garlic, ginger, spices, tomato puree and mushrooms, and fry for a further 5 minutes.

Add the banana and coconut milk, mix well, and simmer for 8-10 minutes, stirring regularly.

Serving suggestions

Serve on a bed of rice with vgf pitta triangles.

Satay Spinach and Sweetcorn

What you need

3 carrots, sliced

2 medium onions, sliced

1 can of sweetcorn, drained

1 can of chickpeas, drained

3 handfuls of spinach

3 tbsp peanut butter

1 tbsp rapeseed oil

200ml water

2 tsp medium curry powder

1 tsp cumin

What to do

Gently fry the onions in the rapeseed oil for 4-5 minutes.

Add the curry powder and cumin and keep stirring for 2 minutes.

Add the carrots, sweetcorn, chickpeas and water and simmer for 15 minutes.

Add the chopped spinach and peanut butter and simmer for 5 minutes.

Serving suggestions

Serve on a bed of rice with vgf pitta triangles

Marmalade Sausages

What you need

1 red pepper, chopped	3 cloves garlic, crushed
1 yellow pepper, chopped	2.5cm fresh ginger, grated
2 onions, chopped	1 tbsp rapeseed oil
1 tbsp tomato puree	300ml vgf stock
2 tbsp orange marmalade	8 vgf sausages

What to do

Cook the vgf sausages as per the instructions on the packet.

Meanwhile, gently fry the onions and peppers in the rapeseed oil for 4-5 minutes. Add the garlic and ginger and fry for a further 2-3 minutes.

Add the tomato puree, marmalade, and stock and simmer for 12-15 minutes.

Pour the marmalade mixture over the cooked vgf sausages.

Serving suggestions

Serve with a baked potato or potato wedges and a nice big roasted tomato which has been drizzled with olive oil, garlic and herbs of your choice.

Coconut Curry

What you need

50g desiccated coconut

2 peppers, sliced

1 red onion, sliced

10-12 baby sweetcorns, halved lengthways

20 mangetout, left whole

20 pea pods, left whole

A handful of spinach, shredded

1 chilli, chopped

3 cloves garlic, crushed

2.5cm fresh ginger, grated

1 can of coconut milk

1 tsp mustard seeds

1 tsp ground cumin

1 tsp cinnamon

What to do

Gently stir fry the onion, peppers, baby sweetcorns, mangetout and peapods in the rapeseed oil for 4-5 minutes.

Add the fresh chilli, garlic, ginger, mustard seeds, cumin and cinnamon, and keep stirring for 2-3 minutes.

Add the tin of coconut milk, the desiccated coconut and spinach, cover the pot and simmer for 10 minutes, stirring regularly.

Serving suggestions

Serve on a bed of brown rice.

Sweet Potato and Aubergine Cottage Pie

What you need

For the topping:

2 large sweet potatoes, peeled and chopped for boiling

1 red onion

For the filling:

300g vgf soya mince, hydrated as per instructions on the packet

1 red pepper, chopped

1 green pepper, chopped

1 aubergine cut into 1.5cm cubes

2.5cm of fresh ginger, grated

400ml of vgf stock mixed with 1 tsp yeast extract, 1 tbsp tomato puree and 2 tsp dried oregano

1 tbsp rapeseed or olive oil

What to do

Boil the sweet potatoes and onion until they are soft enough to mash.

In a separate pot, gently fry the peppers and aubergine in the olive oil until softened. Add the grated ginger and tomato puree and stir-fry for 2 minutes.

Add the stock and soya to the peppers and aubergines. Simmer for 5 minutes and then pour into a baking dish. Cover the mince with the sweet potato topping and bake for 20-25 minutes until nicely browned and bubbling.

Serving suggestions

Serve with lots of garden peas or corn cobs.

Tofu Stir-fry

What you need

2 peppers of your choice, sliced

1 large red onion, sliced

1 broccoli head, broken into small florets

2 carrots, cut into small sticks

20-30 mangetout

12-15 baby corn, halved lengthways

1 pak choi, shredded

1 packet of tofu, cut into 1.5cm cubes

2 tbsp roasted sesame oil

1 tbsp rapeseed oil

1 tbsp soy sauce

2.5cm piece of fresh ginger, grated

3 cloves garlic, crushed

1 tbsp dried oregano

What to do

Place the pieces of tofu on an oiled baking tray and drizzle them with toasted sesame oil. Bake them for 10-15 minutes – turning them over about half way through, adding the soy sauce and a sprinkling of oregano a few minutes before removing from the oven.

Once they are browned, remove them from the oven and put them somewhere to keep warm.

While the tofu is in the oven, stir-fry the onion, broccoli, peppers, baby corns and carrots in rapeseed oil for 15 minutes, covering the pot with its lid in between frequent stirring.

Add the garlic and ginger and continue stirring for 2-3 minutes.

Add additional soy sauce if required.

Serving suggestions

Serve with corn on the cob which has been drizzled with sesame oil and baked at 200°C for 10-12 minutes.

Tofu stir-fry

Houmous Stuffed Peppers

What you need

4 peppers, deseeded and chopped in half lengthways

75g of corn couscous, hydrated

100g mushrooms, finely chopped

8-10 spring onions, finely chopped

1 small can of sweetcorn, drained

100g tofu, mashed

1 small tub of houmous

1 tbsp vegan margarine or 1tbsp rapeseed oil

1tbsp vgf soy sauce

½ tsp paprika

1 tsp mixed herbs

2 garlic cloves, crushed

What to do

Halve the peppers and place them on an oiled baking tray.

Fry the spring onions and mushrooms in the margarine for 4-5 minutes. Add the sweetcorn, tofu, paprika, garlic and soy sauce and keep stirring.

Mix the corn couscous as per the instructions on the packet. Add the hydrated corn couscous and houmous to the pan and mix well. Fill the pepper halves with the mixture.

Bake the now stuffed peppers in an oven at 200°C for 15-20 minutes or until golden brown.

Serving suggestions

Serve with broccoli, carrots and asparagus.

Easy Vegetable Curry

What you need

The florets of 1 small cauliflower

The florets of 1 broccoli

1 medium/large potato, cut into 1.5cm cubes

2 onions, sliced

4 medium carrots, sliced or cubed

1 red chilli, chopped

1 handful of fresh coriander, chopped

250ml vegan cream

1 tbsp sunflower oil

1 tbsp curry powder

2 tsp garlic granules

2 tsp mustard seeds

2 tsp cumin seeds

2 tsp turmeric

What to do

Gently fry the onions and chilli in sunflower oil for about 4-5 minutes until the onions are light brown. Add the garlic powder, turmeric, mustard seeds, cumin seeds and curry powder, and stir into the onions for about 2 minutes.

Add the remaining ingredients, stir, and simmer for 20-25 minutes.

Stir in the vegan cream and simmer for a further 2-3 minutes.

Serving suggestions

Serve with poppadoms, onion salad, and basmati rice.

Lentil Potato Pie

What you need

6 medium white potatoes

200g red lentils, washed

2 onions, finely chopped

1 sweet potato, cubed

2 leeks cut into 1cm pieces

1 tbsp olive oil

1 tbsp vegan margarine

500ml vgf stock

A handful of fresh herbs, chopped (parsley, sage, rosemary, marjoram leaves)

What to do

Boil the potatoes for about 20 minutes until they are soft enough to mash. Mash them.

In a separate pot, gently fry the onions in the olive oil until softened. Add the sweet potato, carrots and vgf stock and stir for 2-3 minutes. Add the lentils and simmer for about 10 minutes.

Mash the boiled potatoes with the herbs and vegan margarine.

Place the carrot/lentil mixture in an ovenproof casserole dish. Spread the herby potatoes over the lentil mixture and bake in an oven at 200°C for 25-30 minutes, or until the top has browned and the lentil mixture is bubbling.

Serving suggestions

Serve with mixed, steamed vegetables.

Nutty Spaghetti

What you need

400g brown rice spaghetti, cooked as per the instructions on the packet

50g pine nuts

50g flaked almonds

100g cashew nuts

2 brown onions, finely chopped

1 leek, finely chopped

3 tbsp olive oil

3-4 crushed garlic cloves

A handful of fresh mixed herbs, finely chopped

Pinch of salt and ground black pepper to taste

100g vegan cheese, grated (optional)

What to do

Cook the brown rice spaghetti as directed on the packet.

Meanwhile, fry the onion and leeks for 5-6 minutes until softened.

Add the pine nuts, flaked almonds, cashews, garlic and herbs to the onions, and keep on the heat for another 3-4 minutes, stirring frequently to prevent the nuts or garlic from burning.

Toss the cooked spaghetti in the nut mixture (and grated vegan cheese if required) and serve.

Serving suggestions

Serve with vgf garlic bread and sprinkle nutritional yeast over the spaghetti.

Spicy Bean Baked Tatties

What you need

4 large baked potatoes

1 can of black-eyed beans, drained

1 can of green lentils, drained

1 can of kidney beans, drained

2 medium red onions, chopped

15-20 cherry tomatoes, halved

4 garlic cloves blended into a paste with 3cm of fresh ginger, grated

4 tbsp olive oil

1 tbsp agave nectar

2 tbsp tomato puree

1 tsp cumin, 1 tsp cinnamon, 1 tbsp curry powder

1 handful of fresh coriander, chopped

What to do

Clean and prick the potatoes and bake for 1-1.5 hours at 200 degrees Centigrade.

Meanwhile, fry the onion in rapeseed oil until browned, then add the cumin, garlic/ginger puree, cinnamon, tomato puree and curry powder and stir well. Stir in the beans, lentils, tomatoes and lemon juice and gently simmer for 15 minutes. Stir in the coriander and agave nectar and simmer for a few minutes.

When the baked potatoes are cooked, halve them and ladle the spiced beans on top

Serving suggestions

Serve with a dollop of vegan yogurt.

Leek Patties

What you need

4-5 medium potatoes, boiled and mashed

200g vegan cheese, grated

4 small slices of vgf brown bread made into breadcrumbs

2 leeks, finely chopped

8-10 shallots, finely chopped

6 spring onions, finely chopped

50ml rice milk

1 tbsp sunflower oil

A handful of fresh chives, finely chopped

Salt and pepper to taste.

What to do

Boil the potatoes and mash the rice milk into them.

Meanwhile, fry the onions, leeks and spring onions in the sunflower oil until softened.

Place in a large mixing bowl with all the other ingredients and mix well.

Shape into flat rounds and leave to stand for 20 minutes.

Fry gently in oil until crisp and light brown on both sides.

Serving Suggestions

Serve with a mixed salad or on rolls for a cheesy leek 'burger'.

Leek patties

Vegan Sausage Pasta

What you need

2 red onions, finely chopped	4 cloves of garlic, crushed
2 tbsp tomato puree	1 tsp smoked paprika
1 can of chopped tomatoes	Handful of chopped fresh parsley, basil and oregano
6-8 vgf sausages	
2 tbsp of olive oil	200g vegan pasta of your choice

What to do

Place vgf sausages in the oven, cook as per the manufacturer's instructions and then cut them into 1cm slices. Put them to one side for later on.

Gently fry the onions in the olive oil for 4-5 minutes.

Add the garlic and paprika and fry for a further 2-3 minutes, frequently stirring.

Add the tomato puree, canned tomatoes, vegan sausages, parsley, basil and oregano and simmer for 10-15 minutes.

Meanwhile, cook the vgf pasta as per the instructions on the packet and, once it is cooked, mix with the veggie sausage tomato sauce.

Serving Suggestions

With salad and/or a baked potato.

Mushroom Veganoff

What you need

200g of button mushrooms, halved

2 leeks, finely sliced

1 finely chopped onion

2 tsp lemon juice

250ml vegan cream

200ml vegan white wine

1 tsp Dijon mustard

1 tbsp tomato puree

1 tbsp rapeseed or sunflower oil

2 tsp dried oregano

Salt and pepper to taste

What to do

Gently fry the onions and leeks in the oil for 3-4 minutes.

Add the mushrooms and white wine and fry for a further 3-4 minutes.

Stir in the tomato puree, mustard, vegan cream, lemon juice and oregano and simmer for 15 minutes.

Serving Suggestions

Sprinkle with nutritional flakes or grated vegan cheese and serve with vgf garlic bread or potato wedges.

Roasted Vegetable Pasta

What you need

250g of vgf penne pasta

2 red onions, sliced,

2 red peppers, sliced

1 green pepper, sliced

1 yellow pepper, sliced

3 medium courgettes, sliced

200g mushrooms, halved

1 can sweetcorn, drained

300ml of vegan yogurt

3 cloves of garlic, crushed

4 tbsp olive oil

1 tbsp of seeded mustard

What to do

Mix the garlic and olive oil together.

Place all of the vegetables on a baking tray and drizzle the oil and garlic mixture over them.

Bake until browned, turning every few minutes. Meanwhile, cook the vgf pasta as recommended on the packet.

When the vegetables and vgf pasta are ready, mix them together.

Mix the seeded mustard and yogurt together and stir through the pasta.

Serving Suggestions

This is lovely served immediately with vgf garlic bread and salad.

Nutty Layer Bake

What you need

250ml vegan cream

50g chopped hazelnuts

50g flaked almonds

100g cashew nuts, chopped

3 peppers, sliced

2 large red onions, sliced

Potatoes cut into thin slices and parboiled for 5-8 minutes

50g vegan cheese, grated

2 garlic cloves, crushed

2 tbsp olive oil

Rapeseed oil to oil the casserole dish

1 handful of chopped fresh mixed herbs

Salt and pepper to taste

What to do

Oil the casserole dish with the rapeseed oil.

Fry the onions and peppers in the olive oil for 4-5 minutes.

Blend the nuts, garlic, herbs, cream and salt and pepper together.

Place alternate layers of the onions and peppers, nutty creamy mixture and parboiled potatoes in the casserole dish, starting and finishing with the parboiled potatoes.

Drizzle olive oil and grated vegan cheese over the top of the final layer of potato and place the casserole dish in the centre of the oven for 40 minutes at 200°C – keep covered with foil for the first 20 minutes.

Serving Suggestions

Serve with potato wedges, broccoli and garden peas.

Soya Bolognese

What you need

1 packet of mushrooms and/or 3 baby courgettes, sliced

2 onions, finely chopped

400g vgf soya mince

1 can of chopped tomatoes

3 garlic cloves, chopped

1 tbsp tomato puree

2 tbsp olive oil

500ml vgf stock

150ml vegan red wine

Handful of chopped fresh flat leaf parsley

What to do

Gently fry the onions in olive oil for 4-5 minutes and add the garlic, tomato puree and wine and fry for another 1-2 minutes.

Add the mushrooms (+/- courgettes) and soya mince and stir fry for 3-4 minutes.

Add the vegetable stock and simmer for 12-15 minutes. Add the parsley and simmer for another 2-3 minutes.

Serving Suggestions

Serve with vgf pasta and sprinkle with nutritional yeast flakes, vegan parmesan, or vegan cheese, grated.

Champ Cottage Pie

What you need

For the potato topping:

6 medium potatoes, peeled and quartered ready for boiling

8 spring onions, finely chopped

200ml rice milk

Salt and pepper to taste

For the filling:

300g vgf soya mince, hydrated as per the packet instructions

4 medium carrots, sliced

3 medium onions, sliced

1 mug of frozen garden peas

2 handfuls of spinach, shredded

1 handful of fine beans cut into 1.5cm pieces

700ml of vgf stock

300ml of ginger beer

1 tsp mustard

2 tbsp olive oil

1 tbsp tomato puree

1 tsp vgf yeast extract

A handful of mixed fresh herbs (parsley, oregano, marjoram)

What to do

Boil the potatoes in water for 20-25 minutes until soft enough to mash.

Meanwhile, add the spring onions and salt and pepper to the rice milk, bring to the boil and simmer for 5 minutes – leave the resulting mixture to one side until the potatoes are ready.

In a separate large pot, gently fry the onions in olive oil until softened. Add the vgf soya mince, carrots, peas, beans, spinach, ginger beer, yeast extract, mustard, tomato puree and vgf stock, cover the pot and simmer for 15 minutes.

Pour the soya mixture into an oven proof dish.

Mash the potatoes and mix them with the spring onions/rice milk, and then carefully spread the potato/onion mixture over the top of the soya base.

Bake for 25-30 minutes at 200ºC.

Serving Suggestions

Serve with boiled sweetcorn and broccoli.

Bean Chilli Bake

What you need

1 medium onion, chopped

2 peppers, chopped

1 can of black-eyed beans, drained

1 can of kidney beans, drained

1 can of chopped tomatoes

1 tbsp tomato puree

2 tbsp rapeseed oil

2.5cm piece of ginger, grated

4 crushed garlic cloves

½-1 tsp chilli flakes

A few coriander leaves, chopped

For the garlic bread and topping

6-8 slices of vgf brown bread made into breadcrumbs

4 more crushed garlic cloves

2 tbsp of olive oil

Handful of finely chopped parsley and oregano, or a teaspoonful of each if dried

What to do

Gently fry the chopped onion and peppers in the rapeseed oil for 4-5 minutes until softened.

Stir in the chilli, garlic and ginger and stir for a further 1-2 minutes.

Add the remaining chilli ingredients and

simmer for 15 minutes.

Meanwhile, mix the olive oil, garlic and herbs together and spread over the slices of vgf bread. Cut the bread into quarters.

Place the chilli in a baking dish.

Arrange the vgf garlic bread over the top of the bean chilli until the chilli is well covered.

Bake in a preheated oven at 200°C for 15-20 minutes until the bread is nicely toasted and the chilli bubbling (keep covered for the first 10 minutes to prevent the bread from burning).

Serving Suggestions

Serve with a baked potato, rice, corn couscous, or vegetables

For a **lentil bake**, simply replace the kidney beans with a can of lentils. If you want a cheesy topping, simply add a sprinkling of grated vegan cheese to the top of the vgf garlic bread about 10 minutes before baking is finished.

Garlic Spinach

What you need

3 medium red onions, chopped

A little rapeseed oil for frying

1 tin of chopped tomatoes

1 tsp of mustard seeds

8 handfuls of spinach, roughly chopped

1 tsp of ground cumin

1 tsp of ground cinnamon

1 tbsp of rapeseed oil

6 cloves of garlic, crushed

2.5cm fresh ginger, grated

What to do

Gently fry the onions in the rapeseed oil for 4-5 minutes.

Add the garlic, ginger and spices and keep stirring for 2 minutes.

Add the tin of chopped tomatoes and the spinach to the pot and simmer for 5-10 minutes, until the spinach has wilted and is dark green.

Serving Suggestions

Serve on a bed of brown rice with sesame seeds sprinkled on the top and vgf pitta bread, or vgf pizza slices which have been coated in a garlic/herb spread and baked for 8-10 minutes.

Hearty Bean Stew

What you need

2 courgettes, sliced

2 medium carrots, sliced

1 medium sweet potato, diced

8-10 spring onions, finely chopped

2 medium onions, sliced

1 can of kidney beans, drained

1 can of butter beans, drained

1 can of chopped tomatoes

500ml vgf stock

1 tsp turmeric

2 tsp paprika

2 tbsp olive oil

What to do

Fry the onion and spring onions in the olive oil for about 4-5 minutes.

Mix in the turmeric and paprika and keep on stirring.

Add the carrots, sweet potato and vgf stock and stir well. Simmer for 8-10 minutes.

Add the drained beans and cover the pot and simmer for 10-15 minutes, removing the lid regularly to stir thoroughly.

Serving Suggestions

Serve with a baked potato, vgf garlic bread or brown rice.

Side Salads

Mixed Bean Salad

What you need

1 can of mixed beans, drained and washed

1 can of sweetcorn, drained and washed

20-25 cherry tomatoes, halved

8 spring onions, chopped into 1 cm pieces

About 20-30 red grapes, halved

For the dressing:

2 tbsp olive oil

1 tsp lemon juice

1 tbsp vegan cider vinegar

1 tbsp agave nectar or maple syrup

What to do

Drain the mixed beans and sweetcorn, wash them in cold water, and tip them into a serving bowl.

Add the chopped tomatoes, grapes, and chopped onions.

Place all of the dressing ingredients in a jar and shake well until mixed thoroughly.

Mix the dressing through the bean salad and serve.

Serving suggestions

Can be a light meal on its own with some warmed vgf bread rolls, or with a baked potato or sweet potato wedges for something a little more substantial.

Spicy Tomato Salad

What you need

20 cherry tomatoes, halved

2 large mild onions, chopped

Half a large cucumber cut into 1cm cubes

2 tbsp of chopped fresh coriander

For the dressing:

4 tbsp of olive oil

2 tbsp of rice vinegar

1 tsp of wholegrain mustard

1tbsp of agave nectar

1 tsp of lemon juice

½ tsp of chilli powder

1 tsp of ground cinnamon

Salt and black pepper to taste

What to do

Place the tomatoes in a serving dish and mix with the onions and cucumber.

Place all the dressing ingredients in a jar and shake until they are thoroughly mixed.

Drizzle the dressing over the salad and sprinkle the coriander over the top.

Serving suggestions

Serve as a side dish with curries.

Balsamic Ciabatta and Olive Salad

What you need

2 vgf ciabatta rolls cut into 2cm pieces

20 baby tomatoes, halved

2 peppers of your choice, sliced

1 can of sweetcorn, washed and drained

1 red onion, thinly sliced

20-30 green or black olives, halved or sliced

Half an iceberg lettuce, shredded

For the dressing:

2 cloves of garlic, chopped

A small handful of fresh, chopped basil

4 tbsp extra virgin olive oil

2 tbsp balsamic vinegar

2 tsp wholegrain mustard

1tbsp agave nectar

What to do

Place all of the dressing ingredients in a jar and shake until they are thoroughly mixed.

Place the chopped vgf ciabatta rolls in a serving dish and drizzle on the dressing – mix well until the ciabatta is quite well coated.

Add the tomatoes, sweetcorn, peppers, olives and onion and toss the salad thoroughly with some salad servers.

Serving suggestions

Serve as an accompaniment to pasta dishes.

Balsamic Ciabatta and Olive Salad

Grape and Cranberry Creamy Salad

What you need

100g dried cranberries (the ones sweetened with juice, not sugar)

20-30 grapes, halved

2 apples cut into 1 cm cubes

1 iceberg lettuce, shredded

2 handfuls of spinach, shredded

50g mixed sunflower and pumpkin seeds

For the dressing

3 tbsp olive oil

The juice of 1 lemon

200ml vegan single cream

1 tsp Dijon mustard

1 tbsp agave nectar

Vegan parmesan to sprinkle over the salad once it is prepared

What to do

Place all the fruit and salad ingredients in a large bowl.

Sprinkle vegan parmesan, sunflower and pumpkin seeds, and the dressing over the top of the salad.

Toss the salad with salad servers and serve immediately.

Serving suggestions

Serve on its own for a nice, light summer lunch.

Apple, Walnut and Warm Potato Salad

What you need

1 iceberg lettuce, chopped

100g walnut halves

100g pecan nuts

15-20 baby potatoes

2 handfuls of spinach, chopped

2 apples, cored and cubed

15cm cucumber, chopped into 1cm cubes

2 vgf ciabatta rolls, cut into 2cm cubes

For the dressing:

100ml soya cream

50ml vegan mayonnaise

The juice of 1 lemon

1tbsp agave nectar

1 tsp Dijon or wholegrain mustard

What to do

Mix all the dressing ingredients together in a jar and shake well.

Bake the baby potatoes at 200ºC for 30-40 minutes until nice and soft.

Place the lettuce, walnuts, pecan nuts, celery and apple in a salad bowl. Drizzle on the dressing and toss well with salad servers. Add the warm baby potatoes.

Serving suggestions

Serve with pasta, rice, or baked potato dishes.

Yellow Pasta Salad

What you need

1 tin of pineapple rings, cut into 1cm pieces (or a fresh pineapple if in season)

50ml of pineapple juice (from the can of pineapple, or from a carton if using fresh pineapple)

1 yellow pepper, chopped

1 tin of sweetcorn, washed and drained

2 tbsp vegan mayonnaise

150g of vgf pasta, prepared as per the packet instructions.

Salt and pepper to taste

What to do

Cook the vgf pasta of your choice as recommended on the packet.

Meanwhile, place the chopped pineapple, sweetcorn and pepper in a bowl with the mayonnaise and pineapple juice.

Once the pasta is drained, add it to the bowl and mix thoroughly, coating it with the mayonnaise.

Leave the pasta salad to cool, tossing it again once ready to serve. Add salt and pepper if you wish.

Serving suggestions

Serve with potato wedges, baked potato dishes, other salads or vgf garlic bread.

Something Sweet

Very Banana and Almond Bread

What you need

5 small, spotty, brown bananas, mashed (or 4 medium or 3 large)

300g gf SR flour

50g unrefined caster sugar

½ tsp baking powder

¼ tsp almond essence

50g flaked almonds

3tbsp rapeseed oil

100ml rice milk

What to do

Mash the bananas and then mix in all the other ingredients, except for the flaked almonds.

Once the mixture is nice and smooth, spoon-mix in the flaked almonds.

Place in a square cake tin for 22-25 minutes in a preheated oven at 210°C, removing it when golden brown, and when the cake is firm to touch.

Serving suggestions

Vegan gluten free ice cream and fruit compote, or simply dusted with some unrefined icing sugar.

Chocolate Banana Cake

What you need

4 ripe bananas, mashed (or 3 medium), mashed

300g gf SR flour

100g unrefined caster sugar

100g cocoa powder

½ tsp baking powder

1 tsp bicarbonate of soda

¼ tsp of salt

2 dstsp cider vinegar

3 tbsp rapeseed oil

250ml rice milk

For the icing:

100g 70% vegan dark chocolate

100g unrefined icing sugar

50g cocoa powder

100ml soya cream

Dairy-free white chocolate buttons to decorate

What to do

Mash the bananas and then mix in all the other sponge ingredients.

Once the mixture is nice and smooth, split it evenly between two 7" round baking tins.

Place in a preheated oven at 210ºC for approximately 20 minutes, removing them when they are firm.

Meanwhile, gently heat the chocolate and

soya cream for the topping in a small saucepan, taking care not to burn it. Stir well throughout until the chocolate has melted. Add the icing sugar and cocoa and mix well until it is a lovely chocolatey paste.

Once the two sponges have cooled, spread half of the icing between them and the other half on the top.

Add some vegan white chocolate buttons for decoration.

Serving suggestions

Vegan gluten free ice cream and fruit compote, or simply dusted with some unrefined icing sugar.

Chocolate and Vanilla Swirl Cake

What you need

300g gf SR flour

100g unrefined caster sugar

1 tsp baking powder

½ tsp bicarbonate of soda

Pinch of salt

2 dstsp cider vinegar

185g jar of apple sauce

200ml rice milk + separate 50ml

2 dstsp rapeseed oil

½ tsp vanilla essence

100g cocoa powder

For the fillings:

Jam of your choice

Vegan butter icing for both

What to do

Mix all the sponge ingredients together (except the vanilla essence, cocoa and the 50ml rice milk).

Split the mixture between two mixing bowls and add the vanilla to one of them and the cocoa and the other 50ml of rice milk to the other. Mix both well.

Place a layer of each in an oiled 7" cake tin and then swirl with a knife to slightly mix the colours.

Bake for 20-22 minutes at 200 degrees Centigrade.

Once cooled they are ready to fill with your choice of fillings. Add a topping of melted chocolate or chocolate/vanilla icing if you wish.

Serving suggestions

Vegan gluten free ice cream and fruit compote, or simply dusted with some unrefined icing sugar

Chocolate and Vanilla Swirl Cake

Cranberry, Lemon and Lime Cheesecake

What you need

Topping:

A packet of silken tofu

2 dstsp of lime juice

1dstsp of lemon juice

The zest from one lemon and one lime

50g caster sugar

50g desiccated coconut

+ chopped hazelnuts to decorate

For the base:

100g cranberries

50g pitted dates

50g pecan nuts

100g cashew nuts

3dstsp agave nectar

What to do

Heat and simmer the topping ingredients (except the coconut) until smooth. Add the coconut and keep on stirring.

Leave the mixture to cool a little while you make the base.

For the base, mix all ingredients in a food blender and then press into a 7" collapsible cake tin. Spread the topping over and sprinkle with chopped hazelnuts. Once properly cool, place the cake in the fridge for 3-4 hours until serving.

Serving suggestions

Dust with vegan icing sugar and serve with vgf vanilla ice cream.

Chocolate Chip Cheesecake

What you need

Topping:

200g of coconut-based vegan gluten free cream cheese

2 dstsp agave nectar

50g cocoa

100g dark chocolate broken into small chocolate chips (or use 50g cacao nibs)

For the base:

8 toffee popcorn rice cakes

100g pecan nuts

2 dstsp agave nectar

2 dstsp vegan gluten free chocolate spread

What to do

Mix the vegan cream cheese, agave nectar and cocoa in a blender. Remove from the blender and put into a bowl and add the chocolate chips (or cacao nibs). Mix well.

Put the topping to one side while you make the base.

Mix all of the base ingredients in a blender and press them into a 7" cake tin.

Spread the topping on top of the base and coat with some grated chocolate for an extra chocolate fix.

Refrigerate for 3-4 hours before serving.

Serving suggestions

Add ½ tsp of peppermint essence to make the topping minty – or use minty chocolate!

Pancakes

What you need

Makes 8 (12-15cm) pancakes

300g plain gluten free flour

2 tbsp unrefined caster sugar

1 tsp baking powder

Pinch of salt

3 tbsp rapeseed oil

500ml rice milk

Rapeseed oil for frying

What to do

Place all the dry ingredients into a mixing bowl.

Add the oil and rice milk and mix well.

Heat some oil in a pan and add about 1/8th of the mixture to the pan.

Fry well on each side and repeat with the other pancakes. Keep the cooked pancakes warm while you fry the rest.

.Serving suggestions

The usual lemon juice and sugar/agave nectar/maple syrup/fruit compote or, (if you're my husband anyway) marmalade!

Avocado Chocolate Torte

What you need

For the topping

Flesh of 2 avocados

2 tbsp smooth peanut butter

6 dstp agave nectar

50g cocoa powder

100g dark vegan chocolate, melted

100ml rice milk

½ tsp vanilla extract

For the base

50g sunflower seeds

50g almonds

100g cashew nuts

2dstp cocoa powder

3dstsp agave nectar

1 tsp vanilla extract

What to do

Place all of the base ingredients into a food mixer and blend until quite stiffly mixed together.

Press the mixture into a lightly-oiled 7" cake tin.

Blend the topping ingredients until they are nice and smooth.

Melt the chocolate and add to the mixture – blend again.

Spread the topping over the base (smooth or peaked).

Place in the freezer for 2 hours.

Remove from the freezer and take out of the baking tin – it should come out easily.

If not ready to serve, place back in the freezer and bring back out 2-3 hours before serving.

Serving suggestions

Serve with nectarine and strawberry compote (The flesh of 3 nectarines, chopped, about 10 medium strawberries, topped and sliced, 2 tbsp unrefined caster sugar, 2 tbsp water – simmer them all together for about 15 minutes, stirring regularly). Serve cold with the torte.

Chocolate avocado torte

Avocoffee and Hazelnut Cake

What you need

Syrupy coffee - ½ mugful made with 2 tsp coffee and 2 tbsp of unrefined sugar

50g chopped hazelnuts

200ml vegan cream

200g gluten free SR flour

1 tsp baking powder

3 avocadoes, peeled and chopped

What to do

Place all the ingredients into a food mixer and blend until they are well mixed together

Press the mixture into a lightly oiled rectangular small loaf-style cake tin.

Bake at 200 degrees Centigrade for 15-20 minutes until it is firm to touch.

Serving suggestions

Serve once cooled with vegan ice cream and/or fruit compote and vegan cream.

Vanilla and Sesame Coffee Cake

What you need

For the cake:

3 tsp coffee in a mug of hot water

100g unrefined fine caster sugar

300g gluten free SR flour

1 tsp baking powder

½ tsp bicarbonate of soda

2 tbsp rapeseed oil

2 tbsp sesame seeds

½ tsp vanilla essence

For the icing:

250g unrefined icing sugar

50g vegan margarine

1 tsp coffee mixed with a tsp of water

¼ tsp vanilla essence

What to do

Place all the cake ingredients into a food blender and blend until quite stiffly mixed together. Press the mixture into a lightly oiled square cake tin and bake at 200 degrees Centigrade for 15-20 minutes.

This will rise only about 3cm. Once cool, coat the cake with the icing and decorate with walnuts or vegan chocolate buttons (or both!).

Serving suggestions

Serve with vegan ice cream or vegan cream.

Coconut Fruit Brulee

What you need

300g fresh strawberries, sliced

300g fresh red grapes, halved

2 nectarines, peeled and cut into small pieces

1 tin of raspberries, drained

250ml vegan cream

250ml vegan yogurt

250ml vegan cream

250ml vegan yogurt

½ mug of desiccated coconut

1 tbsp unrefined caster sugar

What to do

Arrange the fruit in a heatproof dish.

Drain the tinned raspberries and arrange them over the strawberries, nectarines and grapes.

Mix the vegan cream, vegan yogurt and coconut together in a food mixer and pour it over the fruit.

Sprinkle the sugar over the cream/yogurt mixture.

Grill until the sugar is caramelized (use a gas torch if you have one!)

Serving suggestions

Once cooled, serve on its own, but you could serve with some vegan ice cream

Lemon Drizzle Cake

What you need

For the sponge:

300g gluten free SR flour

150g unrefined sugar

A small jar of apple sauce

3tbsp rapeseed oil

300ml soya milk (or can use rice or almond milk)

½ tsp vanilla essence

1tsp xanthan gum

½ tsp bicarbonate of soda

½ tsp baking soda

For the icing drizzle:

Juice and zest of two lemons

100g unrefined icing sugar

What to do

Place all of the sponge ingredients into a bowl and mix well until quite smooth. Pour the mixture into a lined and lightly-oiled square cake tin.

Bake for 20-25 minutes. Meanwhile, mix the icing ready to put the drizzle on the cake.

Once almost cooked, carefully pierce the cake with holes and drizzle. Bake for another 2-3 minutes.

Serving suggestions

Serve with vegan ice cream or vegan cream and fruit compote.

Easy Lemony Cake

What you need

250g gluten free SR flour

200g caster sugar

1 tsp baking powder

1tsp bicarbonate of soda

Juice of ½ lemon + rind of whole lemon

Small 185g jar apple sauce

100ml rapeseed or sunflower oil

200ml water

What to do

Place all of the ingredients in a mixing bowl.

Mix well until it makes a smooth batter.

Place in a square, lightly-oiled cake tin and bake for 20 minutes at 200 degrees Centigrade.

Leave to cool and dust with unrefined icing sugar before serving.

Serving suggestions

Serve on its own with a nice mug of tea or coffee or for a little more indulgence, with vegan cream or a dollop of jam or compote.

Carrot Cake

What you need

For the sponge:

200g rice flour

3 dstsp ground flax

100g coconut sugar

1 ½ tsp baking powder

1 tsp bicarbonate of soda

1 tsp ground cinnamon

200ml almond or soya milk

Small 185g jar of apple sauce

1 small banana mashed

50g ground almonds

200g peeled, finely grated carrots (about 2 medium-sized carrots)

(Optional 50g broken pecans or 50g broken walnuts or 50g sultanas)

Creamy frosting:

150g plain vegan cream cheese

100g unrefined icing sugar

1 tsp water or lemon juice

What to do

Place all of the dry sponge ingredients and plant milk in a mixing bowl and blend well until it forms a thick batter.

Add the apple sauce, mashed banana and grated carrot and mix well.

If adding optional ingredients, mix them through the batter now.

Divide the mixture between two 7" cake tins

and bake at 200 degrees Centigrade for 20-25 minutes until the sponges are firm to touch

Turn out onto a cooling tray, and once cool fill and top with the creamy icing.

Serving suggestions

Delicious on its own but vegan cream, vegan ice cream or fruit compote will never go amiss!

Banana Toffee Pie

What you need

For the base

100g of raw pecan nuts

100g of raw gf oats

50 ml of coconut oil, melted

2 tbsp maple syrup

A little water (if you need it)

For the filling

150g of pitted dates

3 tbsp of smooth cashew butter

1 tsp lemon juice

Pinch salt

3 bananas sliced

For 'cream':

2 cans of coconut milk (drain off the fluid, just need the creamy part)

2 dstsp of the toffee filling mixture

(mix them all together)

Dark chocolate – 2 squares grated – for the top

1 tsp vanilla essence

3 tbsp water

Save a bit of the filling

What to do

Food process the base ingredients and press them into a square cake tin. Bake the base for about 10 minutes at 200 degrees Centigrade, making sure you don't burn it.

Meanwhile, mix the topping ingredients in a blender until smooth.

Once the base is cooled, arrange the sliced bananas over it.

Pour the toffee topping over the bananas, keeping about 2 dstsp of it to make the cream.

Mix the creamy parts (only the solid white part, pour off the water) of the two cans of coconut milk in the blender with the toffee mixture.

Spread the toffee cream over the toffee filling and grate vegan dark chocolate over the top.

Serving suggestions

This is a much easier recipe than it might seem and is delicious on its own or with vegan ice cream.

Choc-nut Cheesecake

What you need

For the topping

1½ packets of plain vegan cream cheese

150g vegan dark chocolate

50g of chopped hazelnuts

50g cocoa

50g unrefined icing sugar

1 tbsp maple syrup

100ml of soya cream

For the base:

12 vgf oat biscuits, crushed

2 tbsp vegan margarine

1 tbsp maple syrup

50g sunflower seeds

What to do

For the base, gently melt the margarine in a saucepan over a low heat. Once melted, add the oat biscuits, sunflower seeds and maple syrup and mix well. Press the mixture into a 7" cake tin.

For the topping, gently melt the chocolate with the soya cream over a low heat. Add the other tbsp of maple syrup and chopped nuts and stir well. Using a blender, mix the remaining topping ingredients together. Mix this mixture with the nutty melted chocolate and spread over the base. Refrigerate.

Serving suggestions

After 2-3 hours, serve with vegan cream.

Fruit, Nut and Chocolate Fondue

What you need

200g vegan chocolate

250ml soya or rice cream

25g cocoa powder

2 tbsp maple syrup

Fruit of your choice, but especially good with dried apricots, Brazil nuts, fresh strawberries and cubes or sticks of fresh pineapple

What to do

Gently melt the chocolate in a saucepan and then stir in the soya cream and maple syrup.

Remove from the heat and add the cocoa – keep on mixing until smooth.

Serve immediately in small individual bowls on a plate with fruit and nuts around each person's bowl.

Serving suggestions

Serve with chopped nuts and desiccated coconut as optional extras.

For some extra nutty crunch, try mixing some chopped hazelnuts into the chocolate sauce.

The sauce is smooth enough to serve in bowls – you don't need a fondue set!

Mango and Strawberry Sorbet

What you need

400g strawberries, washed and quartered

2 medium – sized mangoes , peeled, cored and chopped into pieces

250g unrefined caster sugar

250ml water

Juice of two lemons

What to do

Blend the mangoes and strawberries in a food blender.

Place the blended mangoes and strawberries in a saucepan with all the other ingredients and simmer for about 5 minutes, stirring regularly.

Pour into a suitable container and leave to cool with the lid off, stirring regularly.

Once cool enough to put in the freezer, stir again, and place the lid on the container.

Remove the sorbet from the freezer every hour or so and give it a good stir – it takes about 10-12 hours to set properly (but will be faster in a fast-freeze).

Serving suggestions

While it does take a while to set, it is massively worth it. I love it – it is my favourite sorbet – serve with compote or grated chocolate.

Banana Walnut Cake

What you need

2 medium bananas, mashed

300g rice flour

100g unrefined caster sugar

½ tsp bicarbonate of soda

1 tsp baking powder

2 dstsp ground flaxseeds

100g broken walnuts

¼ tsp salt

2 dstsp cider vinegar

250 ml plant milk (I used almond)

2 tsp coffee mixed with 100ml hot water.

What to do

In a mixing bowl mash the bananas. Add all the other ingredients (except the walnuts) and mix until it is a smooth batter.

Add the walnuts and mix though the batter.

Place in a lightly-oiled square cake tin and bake for approximately 20 minutes at 200 degrees Centigrade.

Serve once cooled.

Serving suggestions

Lovely with a dollop of home-made jam.

Some Snacks to have with a Cuppa

Coffee Biscuits
(Makes 10 - 12 Biscuits)

What you need

250g plain gluten free flour

50g vegan margarine

4 tsp of coffee mixed with 3 dstsp of hot water

1 tsp baking powder

100g unrefined caster sugar

50g ground flaxseed

½ tsp vanilla essence

2 dstsp rice milk

3 dstsp rapeseed oil

What to do

Preheat the oven to 200 degrees.

Mix all the dry ingredients together in a bowl with the margarine. Add the rest of the ingredients. Knead together.

Roll out the dough until it is about ½ cm thick (or roll into balls and then flatten if you want cookie-style biscuits), cut into shapes with a biscuit cutter, and bake on a lightly-oiled baking tray for around fifteen 10-12 minutes.

Serving suggestions

Perfect with a hot mug of vegan cream swirled coffee.

Lemony Coconut Biscuits
(Makes 10 - 12 Biscuits)

What you need

200g plain gluten free flour

50g desiccated coconut

100g unrefined caster sugar

40g ground flaxseed

50g vegan margarine

1 tsp baking powder

3-4 dstsp soya or rice milk

2 dstsp rapeseed oil

The rind and juice of 2 lemons

What to do

Preheat the oven to 200 degrees.

Mix all the dry ingredients together in a bowl with the margarine. Add the rest of the ingredients. Knead together and make into a dough. Depending on how much lemon juice is squeezed from the lemons, it may make a wet dough – if so just mix in a little more plain gluten free flour.

Roll the dough out until it is about ½ cm thick, cut into shapes with a biscuit cutter (or roll into balls and squash into cookie shapes), and bake on a lightly-oiled baking tray for around fifteen 14-16 minutes – until lightly browned.

Serving suggestions

Lovely with lemon or ginger tea or a good brew of breakfast tea.

Peanut Cookies
(Makes 12 - 14 Biscuits)

What you need

4 dstsp peanut butter (crunchy if you like)

3 generous dstsp vegan margarine

100g coconut sugar

200g plain gluten free flour

1 tsp bicarbonate of soda

1 tsp baking powder

50g ground flaxseed

3-4 dstsp cold water

Pinch salt

What to do

Preheat the oven to 200 degrees.

Mix all the dry ingredients together in a bowl with the margarine. Add the rest of the ingredients. Knead together and make into a dough.

Roll the dough out until it is about ½ cm thick, cut into shapes with a biscuit cutter (or roll into balls and squash into cookie shapes), and bake on a lightly-oiled baking tray for around fifteen 10-12 minutes – until lightly browned.

Serving suggestions

Just great with anything!

Chocolate Shortbread
(Makes 10 - 12 Biscuits)

What you need

200g plain gluten free flour

50g vegan margarine

100g coconut sugar

50g cocoa

50g ground almonds

50g ground flaxseed

1 tsp baking powder

Pinch of salt

4 dstsp soya milk

3 dstsp rapeseed oil

3 dstsp maple syrup

What to do

Preheat the oven to 200 degrees.

Mix all the dry ingredients together in a bowl with the margarine. Add the rest of the ingredients. Mix together and make into a dough.

Roll the dough out until it is about ½ cm thick, cut into shapes with a biscuit cutter, and bake on a lightly-oiled baking tray for around fifteen 10-12 minutes – until lightly browned.

Serving suggestions

Great on a cold winter's night with a nice big mug of vgf hot chocolate.

Choc Chip Orange Cookies
(Makes 8 - 10 cookies)

What you need

200g plain gluten free flour

100g unrefined caster sugar

50g cocoa

50g ground flaxseed

50g ground almonds

1 tsp baking powder

50g of vegan chocolate chips (or use cacao nibs)

50g vegan margarine

2 dstsp agave nectar

4 dstsp rice milk

3 dstsp rapeseed oil

½ tsp orange essence

Zest from 2 oranges

Juice of ½ an orange

What to do

Preheat the oven to 200 degrees.

Mix all the dry ingredients together in a bowl with the margarine. Add the rest of the ingredients. Mix together and then knead into a dough.

Roll into balls and flatten into cookie shapes, then bake on a lightly-oiled baking tray for around fifteen 10-12 minutes – until lightly browned.

Serving suggestions

Has to be with ginger tea!

Choc-Nut Fridge Bake

What you need

100g ground almonds

100g chopped hazelnuts (or whole peanuts)

150g vgf digestive biscuits, crushed

300g dark vegan chocolate

25g vegan margarine

2 dstsp agave nectar

For the topping:

200g vegan chocolate to use as topping (melted with a dstsp agave nectar

What to do

Crush all the biscuits together in a bowl with the end of a rolling pin. Add the nuts and ground almonds to the bowl.

Slowly melt the margarine, agave nectar and 300g chocolate together on the hob, stirring well as it melts. Pour the chocolate mixture over the dry ingredients. Mix together thoroughly.

Firmly press the mixture into a suitably-sized baking tray so the tray bake is about 1.5cm thick. Melt the topping chocolate with the remaining agave nectar and pour it over the chocolate biscuit mixture. Put in a fridge to cool and then cut into squares once nice and firm.

Serving suggestions

Great for when there are coffee mornings and everyone is contributing to the tray bakes, or just for a special movie night in treat.

Coffee cookies, choc-nut fridge bake and cranberry and apricot nut energy balls

Raw Nutty Energy Balls

For energy on the go!

Simple recipes for the energy balls:

For all the energy balls just put the ingredients in the blender and blend well – then roll into balls and refrigerate:

Cashew Coconut Balls

(Makes 12 - 14)

200g pitted dates

100g desiccated coconut

100g cashews

50g sunflower seeds

50g walnut pieces

4 dstsp agave nectar

2dstsp cocoa or cacao

Cranberry Balls

(Makes 10 - 12)

150g cranberries

100g cashew nuts

100g walnuts

100g desiccated coconut

4 dstsp agave nectar

2 dstsp cacao or cacao nibs (the nibs give them a crunchy texture and the cacao makes them chocolatey, or just use ordinary cocoa.

Apricot Nut Balls

(Makes 10 - 12)

50g ground almonds

200g dried apricots (orange ones)

100g of cashew nuts

50g of chopped hazelnuts

50g desiccated coconut

Lemon Balls

(Makes About 10)

100g cashew nuts

50g raisins

50g cranberries

50g desiccated coconut

Zest and juice of 2 lemons

3 dstsp agave nectar

Mixed Fruit and Nut Balls

(Makes About 16)

100g cashew nuts

50g mixed seeds (I used a mix of linseeds, pumpkin and sunflower seeds)

50g raisins

50g cranberries

100g pecans

50g ground almonds

50g desiccated coconut

4 dstsp of maple syrup

30g of cacao nibs

CONTENTS

Desserts

Very banana and almond bread	124
Chocolate banana cake	125
Chocolate and vanilla swirl cake	127
Cranberry, lemon and lime cheesecake	129
Chocolate chip cheesecake	130
Pancakes	131
Avocado chocolate torte	132
Avocoffee and hazelnut cake	134
Vanilla and sesame coffee cake	135
Coconut fruit brulee	136
Lemon drizzle cake	137
Easy lemony cake	138
Carrot cake	139
Banana toffee pie	140
Choc-nut cheesecake	142
Fruit, nut and chocolate fondue	143
Mango and strawberry sorbet	144
Banana walnut cake	145

Dips

Salsa dip	40
Cucumber dip	40

Energy Balls

Cashew coconut balls	155
Cranberry balls	156
Apricot nut balls	156
Lemon balls	157
Mixed fruit and nut balls	157

Lentil dishes

Rich red wine lentil casserole	69
Lentil chilli corn couscous	70
Lentil potato pie	99

Mushroom dishes

Baked aubergine in a mushroom sauce	58
Mushroom dry curry	72
Mushroom veganoff	105

Nutty dishes

Creamy cashew curly kale	45
Cashew and sunflower bake	46
Nutty vegetable crumble	54
Nutty creamy cauliflower	60
Creamy tomato and almond Vegetables	61
Roasted vegetable nut roast	73
Nutty layer bake	107

Pasta dishes

Sundried tomato pasta	53
Walnut gluten free penne	71
Spinach lasagne	82
Nutty spaghetti	100
Vegan sausage pasta	104
Roasted vegetable pasta	106

Polenta

Polenta and baby tomatoes	39

Quinoa

Pepper, peach and olive quinoa	89

Rice dishes

Shitake, tofu and sesame risotto	43
Pine nut and sweetcorn risotto	65

Chunky stew	75
Soya Bolognese	108
Champ cottage pie	109

Tofu dishes

Ginger and orange chunks	57
VGF all day breakfast	66
Tofu Italia	67
Tofu scramble and spinach on toast	68
Lightly battered tofu	76
Tofu chow mein	77
Sweet and sour tofu	78
Tofu stir fry	95

Vegan sausage dishes

Vegan sauspot	49
Vegan sausage ratatouille	80
Marmalade sausages	92
Vegan sausage pasta	104

Vegetable dishes

Summer vegetable wraps	88
Houmous stuffed peppers	97
Sweet potato and aubergine cottage pie	94

OTHER BOOKS BY CLARE COGBILL

A Dog Like Ralph

. . . A Book for Anyone Who has Ever Loved a Rescue Dog

The true story of Ralph—a rescue dog with a difficult past—who loves other dogs, is frightened of people and cars, and mesmerized by cats, rabbits and 'Santa Please Stop Here' signs. Clare, his new human companion, tells with equal amounts of humour and sadness about the challenges and joys of having him as a companion.

His story is partly told through his eyes and describes how what he may have experienced before has affected how he interacts with those in his new 'forever' home. When Ralph's compatriots, Peggy and Luella (Lucy to her friends), enter his life, it becomes clear that they have their own 'version of events' to add to the story!

Clare also writes about the pitfalls of a society that has resulted in Ralph being the way he is, and of how small changes could transform the plight of abandoned dogs. This book is a tribute to the rescue dog.

A Dog Like Ralph gives some of the back story to *The Diary of a Human and a Dog (or Three)*, but it is not necessary to read *A Dog Like Ralph* first.

A Soldier Like Jack

Like millions of other young men, Jack was plunged into a war which was to change his life, and the lives of his loved ones, forever. Jack's war would take him to Salonika (Thessaloniki), in Greece.

Jack's wife, Grace, tells the harrowing story of what happened to the men and the families they left behind. It traces their lives from the time of Jack and Grace's marriage in 1912, until Grace's death in 1957.

This is a true story based on the lives of the author's great grandparents, Jack and Grace Cogbill.

Lilac Haze

You don't remember your childhood in detail, so your memories thirty or forty years on have become hazy; times you had back then are painted in colours that have become distorted.

This is a love story. In the end, anyway, that's what it will be. A love story gives you hope: whatever you have lost; whatever you have to gain. For me, as someone on daily kidney dialysis, when an offer of a kidney came along which I couldn't possibly refuse, there was everything to gain.

But the past has a way of interfering with what seems to be the right path . . . and how do you ever in this life repay such an immeasurable debt?

The Diary of a Human and a Dog
(or Three)

The story of a human and a dog sharing their unanticipated grief

When a dog loses their human companion it results in the upheaval of everything they've ever loved. When a human loses their parent it is the most heart-rending thing to have to deal with.

Lucy had been rescued just two years earlier and thought she had found her forever home. She was living as the sole dog in charge of an old woman. When the old woman passed away, Lucy found herself thrust into a life in which she would have to share her new humans with two other dogs. She had encountered Ralph and Peggy before and, quite frankly and in her stroppy terrier way, was not that keen on them.

This is the diary of Clare and Lucy. It is a story of how dogs can help humans heal, and how humans can help dogs to overcome their own very special sort of grief.

ABOUT THE AUTHOR

Clare Cogbill was born in the mid-1960s, and like many youngsters from an early age she developed a deep passion for animals and their welfare. She had fifteen years experience of working with domesticated animals in rescue shelters, and as a qualified veterinary nurse in both welfare and private practice environments before, in 1991, becoming a lecturer in animal care and veterinary nursing. These days she mostly teaches companion animal welfare. She has been vegan since 2002 and was vegetarian for 25 years before that. Vegan cookery is one of her greatest passions, and other than when out walking with her dogs, the kitchen is where she feels happy and chilled.

While animals have always been her greatest interest, she also loves to read, preferring biographies to fiction, and where those books contain some reference to the human-animal bond, all the better. She also enjoys reading books that have been made into films, but still can't quite work out whether it's better to read the book or to see the film first!

Clare lives in Scotland with her gluten free vegan husband, three rescue dogs, and two rescued hamsters. She has one vegan son who has now flown the nest and is following his dreams with his vegan partner.

If you've enjoyed any of my books, do please get in touch through Facebook or Goodreads.

Reviews on Amazon and/or Goodreads are very gratefully received.

Dreaming

of a vegan world.

Printed in Great Britain
by Amazon